HOW TO
LIVE ABOVE
YOUR PROBLEMS

HOW TO LIVE ABOVE YOUR PROBLEMS

by

ORAL ROBERTS

FIRST PUBLISHED EDITION

FIRST PRINTING	200,000 SEPTEMBER 1974
SECOND PRINTING	100,000 SEPTEMBER 1974
THIRD PRINTING	100,000 OCTOBER 1974
FOURTH PRINTING	100,000 OCTOBER 1974
FIFTH PRINTING	100,000 NOVEMBER 1974

PRINTED IN THE UNITED STATES OF AMERICA

Contents

Oral Roberts

1

How You Can Live Above The Everyday Problems Of Life

A GROUP OF MY ASSOCIATES and I were sitting around a long table the other day and they began to ask me questions. They were concerned about themselves, also many others who we are trying to help through this ministry. They said, "Brother Roberts . . .

"What do you think about the political situation in America today . . . about the effects of Watergate . . . the credibility gap in government . . . the threat of war that seems constant . . . the trouble our nation is in at this time?"

"What about the inflation we're all facing?"

"What is your feeling about the depression that some people believe will strike America?"

"What about the problem that people seem to be sick more of the time?"

And on and on they went from one question to another until they had covered the range of problems of this nation, and then of individuals facing problems that seem to be getting harder day by day.

I thought about their questions and I examined my heart. I didn't want to cover up . . . to give a phony kind of reply.

I wanted to say something that was welling up within my being. My reply, in essence, was this:

> "I am very concerned about these things you are talking about but I am not remotely concerned about holding them in my mind until they get on top of me. You ask me why? Well, these things are not my Source. MY SOURCE IS GOD. All these situations you've mentioned mean things are not stable, they are changing all the time. You get one of them fixed, and another rises up to bother you. But God doesn't change. He is constant. He is always the same and He is in the NOW."

GOD IS YOUR SOURCE IN GOOD TIMES AND IN BAD TIMES

The men and women sitting around me were reaching out to what I was trying to share, from the Spirit of God within me, with each of them.

One said, "We think we know what you try to practice yourself but will you tell us again?"

I thought of the power of the Seed-Faith concept my Savior has given to each of us if we can understand it and, as my associates said, put it in practice. So I replied out of the depths of all I know about what Jesus has taught me, "As each individual—you, myself, and the partners and friends of this ministry—faces problems we must learn on a personal basis to make God our Source. This means: Try to give God your best, and then boldly ask Him for His best. He's going to take care of you. In good times and in bad times God is going to take care of those who trust in Him. I just feel sorry for people who get up and down about all these different negative conditions and think and worry that these conditions are going to get them down and keep them down. Bad conditions are really going to affect you if you let them do it. But if you let God affect your life, He's going to take care of you. God is bigger than the whole thing—all the shortages and problems in the nation and the world—put together! And more important to you, God is bigger than all the bad things in your own little world."

Then they said, "Well, we are glad that you made that statement."

And I replied, "It's because I believe it. I know it is the truth as God gives it to us in His holy Word!"

Then I pointed out that a Christian who practices Seed-Faith living . . . who *seeds* for a miracle . . . who gives God something to work with through which to receive his miracles . . . is not dependent on whether there is prosperity in the land or not but because he draws from a different supply, a higher power.

I can honestly say I do just as well whether the conditions are high or low because I am not looking to conditions, they are not my Source. I am looking to Him who is above all highs and lows. GOD. I say that with all the sincerity of my being. I say that with the knowing of faith in me. Yes, I am surrounded with the letters I receive . . . and I stand daily in the midst of every kind of need and problem. People are wonderful in sharing with me exactly what they are going through, how lonely and down they often feel, and how they want help. I appreciate this because it causes me to seek God for answers, and it lets me feel how they feel, and it makes me get down to the real Source, our Lord himself.

WHAT GOD REVEALED TO ME IN THE PRAYER TOWER

Not long ago I spent the day in the Prayer Tower reading my mail and praying for the needs of the people. I sat there by myself. I had my Bible. I had my Seed-Faith book. I had the letters and I had the Spirit of God in my life.

People were visiting the Prayer Tower by the hundreds that day. I could see them coming in and going out. I could hear them outside my room. As I meditated and prayed I began to say . . . "Oral Roberts, who is your Source? Is it God, or is it yourself? Or is it the people? Or is it conditions in the world when they are right?"

I had to ask those questions of myself. Then I began to say, "Oral Roberts, are you seeding for miracles? Are you putting seed in for God to work with? Are you expecting many miracles??" While I was doing this—and it took a lot of time—I would pick up 50 to 100 letters from my partners and friends and I would read them. Then I'd put them down and read some more. This went on for several hours.

I found that in about 80% of the letters my friends and partners were pouring out of their hearts things like these:

"Brother Roberts:

"This is what has happened to me . . ."

"This is what I've lost . . ."

"This is what someone has done against me . . ."

"My marriage is in trouble . . ."

"I've lost my job . . ."

"My business is facing trouble . . ."

"The conditions in this country are getting to me. I've become negative. Bad things are happening to me. Pray for me. PRAY FOR ME!!"

"I'm a Christian. I've been a Christian a long time but I've never had it so bad as now."

"I'm a sinner and I don't know how to find God."

"Bills are piling up and I can't meet them."

"Sometimes I feel there is either no God or if there is,

He sure doesn't care anything about me."
"I've gotta' have help and I've gotta' have it now."

Gradually I saw a pattern forming. When I saw the condition of the people I just involuntarily cried out in my heart:

DEAR GOD, WILL YOU USE ME TO COMMUNICATE THE SEED-FAITH PRINCIPLES OF THE BIBLE SO THAT PEOPLE WILL NOT CONTINUE TO LIVE BENEATH THEIR PROBLEMS.

"Lord, let me preach and let me communicate the miracle of Seed-Faith to people so that they will have victory . . . they will have health . . . they will have success . . . and good things will happen more often than bad things . . . so that until the day You take them to a better place than this world they will be in a state of getting their needs met . . . they will have a knowing in their heart that God is going to take care of them."

So in the very first chapter of this book I want to go into this deeper dimension of following Christ in the miracle of Seed-Faith. I shall bare my heart. I shall open the Book of God, the Bible, and I will tell you in plain terms what I believe it means to be a follower of Christ. I want to show you how you can live above your problems, how you can get your needs met and really make your life count.

PLANTING AND REAPING IS AN ETERNAL LAW

I will begin at the beginning . . . with the first book of the Bible. There God says:

> *While the earth remaineth, seedtime and harvest . . . shall not cease* (Genesis 8:22).

God is saying, as long as the earth remains people are going to be planting seed and reaping a harvest. Now that is an eternal law. God is saying there will be an earth and it will abide, and as long as it remains there will be seed-time. That is, there will be a time that you go and plow up the ground and put seed in it. The source is the earth and when you put the seed in the source, the Source will cause the seed to multiply into a harvest. First, seed-time, then a harvest to follow.

God said this in the very beginning and this law is still in operation today. Every time you sow a seed for a flower or plant a garden . . . or whatever you plant in the earth, you have the potential of a harvest. This will be true as long as the earth remains. Now the broader spiritual application of this is that as long as your life remains on earth there will be seed-time and harvest for you. That is, God gives you the privilege to sow seed. The seeds you sow are the things that you give, whether you give of your love or of your hate . . . whether you give of your concern or your unconcern. Remember, there is *good* seed and there is *bad* seed. And every seed, whether good or bad, that you plant will have a harvesttime. From each seed, you will reap. My Bible says:

> *WHATSOEVER a man soweth, that shall he also reap* (Galatians 6:7).

That's plain, isn't it? Whatever you sow will be reaped back by you. But it plainly says something equally true: You cannot reap unless you put seed in. You yourself must plant the seed. That's very important for you to know.

This verse in Galatians 6:7 is meant to be positive and not negative. The emphasis is upon planting seed, good seed, and knowing you SHALL REAP from it.

It contains the secret of how to get your needs met. It tells you that you are capable of sowing that which is good, and from that good seed which you sow God will multiply and bring back to you a return (or a harvest) in the way you need it and when you need it.

But it isn't just a matter of sowing seed once in a while but of continuously sowing . . . of becoming a sow-ER. Let me illustrate: You may go once in a while into your yard or garden or field and dig a hole and put a seed in, but that does not make you a farmer. Or you may give once in a while, but unless you give continuously you do not become a give-ER. You may sow a seed once in a while but that is different from doing it constantly and becoming a sow-ER of seed.

Friend, it is your *attitude* that will make you or break you. It is the *pattern* of your life that will determine the outcome of your existence. Everybody does good things—or sows good seeds—once in a while and that's good, but that's not nearly as good as doing good things all the time. It isn't the same as forming a *pattern* of sowing good seed so that the entire thrust of your life is to sow good seed . . . to do good. Now I don't mean to infer that you won't do something bad now and then, but the bad seed you sow can be very, very small in comparison to the good seed that you sow.

This means Jesus wants you to have an *attitude* of faith—of Seed-Faith. Now what am I saying? I'm saying it's important first to *start* climbing the stairway of the Christian faith, but it's even more important to keep climbing . . . to stay on the stairway. Get a foot on the stairway but don't take it off. Start climbing the stairs one at a time AND KEEP ON CLIMBING.

GET ON THE STAIRWAY AND KEEP CLIMBING

For example, I could climb one step and think I had done well, but I could get off of it. That is, I could come to Christ and then back out and quit. Or I could come to Christ and just keep on, every day trying to have a good attitude, trying to serve Him, to sow good seed. It all boils down to making a DAILY commitment or a dedication—whichever word you want to use—of your LIFE to the Lord and, secondly, a commitment to His way of doing things. It all boils down to BECOMING a follow-ER of Christ. Jesus said:

> *If any man will come after me* (be my follower or learner), *let him deny himself, and take up his cross daily, and follow me* (Luke 9:23).

We have to *learn* who Jesus is. He is a person. He is our Savior. He is our Source. He is the Source of our total supply. We have to follow HIM and learn of HIM. It's awfully easy to look to someone other than Christ and expect them to solve your problems, but it's terrible when they let you down. It's awfully easy to get encouraged when there's prosperity in the land, and things are going good for you . . . and it's easy too to get discouraged when there's depression or recession. But you are wrong and so am I if we look at it that way, because our Source is not the economy. Who is our Source? Jesus. If you can learn this one thing . . . if you can learn who your Source is you are not going to let Watergate, or inflation, or recession, or anything else really bother you. Jesus said:

> *The gates of hell shall not prevail against it* (the church) (Matthew 16:18).

If the hell gate can't do it, Watergate can't do it.

Sometimes we wonder, is God concerned about me? Do you know how I know you ask that question? Because at times I too wonder if God is concerned about me, about my family, about my hopes and dreams. I don't think you are any different than I am. We are both just human beings and we need to be reminded of the truth. When I'm wondering if God cares for me, my wife says, "Oh, Oral, you KNOW God cares for you."

I say, "Does He, Evelyn?"

"Yes."

"Well, say it to me, honey."

"You want me to say it to *you*?"

"Yes. I want you to say it to me. Honey, I've got feelings. I'm a human being."

Sometimes I hurt. Sometimes I get up on the wrong side of the bed. Sometimes I'm sick. My head hurts, or I've got the flu, or a cold, or I just don't feel good some mornings, or the bills are piling up. There are needs I have I can't handle. Sometimes I need somebody to tell me, "God loves you, Oral. God's concerned about you." Everybody needs to know that God cares.

IS GOD INTERESTED IN SMALL THINGS?

I was on a panel the other day after preaching a sermon. On that panel there was a very highly educated man of God. I respect him very much but he and I were at opposite poles in the way we look at God. Here's what happened:

During my sermon I had said, "If you were on the Oral Roberts University campus and it was examination time, you'd see the students going across campus to the classroom. If you were close you would see some of them with their heads kind of down and they would be 'praying in the Spirit.' The reason they would be praying like this would be to quiet their nerves and calm themselves down. They believe the Holy Spirit can quicken their memory so they can make their grades. Not only do they study but they also ask the Holy Spirit to give them some extra help."

I thought it was a wonderful point. Then this fellow's time

came. He got up and said, "I want to tell you two things I don't like. First, a lay person (it was a meeting of pastors and laymen) rushed up to me this morning. She was excited and she said, 'I had a miracle this morning. I lost the buckle off my shoe and it worried me. I liked that buckle and I began to hunt it and couldn't find it. I asked the Lord to help me and I found my buckle and here it is. It's a miracle!'"

He said, "I don't believe in that kind of stuff."

"Second," he said, "I admire Oral Roberts. He has so much influence across America. He really has influence over millions of people. He says his students go across the campus before they have their examinations and they pray so they will make better grades. I don't believe in that. I don't believe that God is concerned about trivial matters and inconsequential things. God is concerned about the world. He's concerned about pollution. He's concerned about civil rights. He's concerned about the big issues. He isn't concerned about whether you lose and find a buckle or whether you pass or fail an examination. One thing I don't like about Oral Roberts is that he's always telling people that God is concerned about every little thing they personally face."

The moderator of the panel turned and said, "Dr. Roberts, please reply to the man."

I just said, "Well, when Jesus had to pay His taxes and didn't have the money He sent one of His disciples, Peter, fishing. He pointed out where he would catch a fish and in that fish's mouth would be money. He told Peter to take that money and pay the taxes. If I didn't know that, and if I didn't know that Jesus said He counted the number of hairs on our head, then I might agree with this man that Jesus is not concerned with what he calls trivial matters. But there was nothing so small and personal that Jesus was not concerned about it when He was on earth. No matter how little it was, whether it was a pain in the body or a pain in the heart or something wrong in the country, He was concerned. I also believe that if this woman who lost a buckle and found it, and these students who pray before they have examinations can have faith for little things like this then maybe when they face something bigger in life, such as cancer or a marriage problem, they can have faith for that."

I had not known what I was going to say until I opened my mouth. When I finished, the audience stood up and cheered. But whether they had cheered or not I knew that I had told the truth. I want to say it again to you . . .

**GOD IS CONCERNED ABOUT YOU . . .
HE IS CONCERNED ABOUT EVERYTHING—
BIG OR SMALL—THAT HAPPENS TO YOU**

Don't ever feel condemned when you read the verse in the Bible where Jesus said, "O ye of little faith," for He is not condemning you . . . He is complimenting you. For if you can have little faith, that faith can grow. And maybe some day you can have big faith.

CHRIST DOESN'T CONDEMN YOU FOR HAVING LITTLE FAITH. HE JUST WANTS YOU TO HAVE *SOME* FAITH.

If you can just take one step and get on the stairway maybe you can have faith to take another step. Maybe you can climb all the way. Don't ever despise the fact that you can only believe for something very small in your life. Maybe some day there will be something bigger you need to believe for and then you can believe for that. Jesus said:

If ye have faith as a grain of mustard seed, ye shall say unto this mountain, Remove hence to yonder

> *place; and it shall remove; and nothing shall be impossible unto you* (Matthew 17:20).

Now *what* did Jesus say you need to have?

FAITH . . . AS A LITTLE SEED. If you have faith *as a little seed* you can *say* . . . and *what* do you talk to??

The MOUNTAIN.

Now I want you to notice, friend, the order in which Jesus places what you are to do.

First, you put the seed in.

Second, you talk to the mountain.

Ordinarily we talk to the mountain *first*. Do you know why? Because it represents our need, our problem, and it hurts the worst. If your leg is hurting, that's uppermost in your mind. It's a mountain to you, isn't it? If you're sick, that's a mountain and you wish the sickness would get out of you right now, if not sooner. If you don't have a job, that's a mountain to you and you are concerned about the mountain. If you've got trouble in your marriage, that's a mountain to you. If finances are not what they should be with you, that's a mountain to you. If you are not getting along with somebody, that's a mountain to you. If you are not growing spiritually, that's a mountain to you. Whatever is wrong is a mountain, and that's where your mind is. How do I know this? Because that's where my mind is too much of the time. My mind is too much on the mountain. But I have to reeducate myself and *learn God's way of doing things. And how does He do things?* Jesus tells me that if I have courage to put a seed in first I then can begin to cope with the mountain. If I think about the mountain first it's going to get on top of me and then I'm really in trouble. In fact, this happens sometimes. Sometimes my problems get so great to me that my mind can't handle them. Sometimes, I wish I never had been born. But if I have the courage to put the seed in, then I can have the faith to talk to the mountain and tell it to get out of my life. I tell you, Jesus is right. It's a lot easier to put that seed in than it is to wrestle with that big mountain.

LEARN JESUS' WAY OF DOING THINGS

Friend, our Lord is saying something very valuable to you. He's telling you something precious. I am spending my life trying to learn it, and to learn it better and better, and I believe I'm doing it. What is it I'm trying to learn? TO LEARN JESUS' WAY OF DOING THINGS. It is so good to have Jesus as the Lord of your life, the Head of your life, the Source of your life, to put Him first, but if you don't know the way of the Lord . . . if you don't know the way God does things . . . then that may be the reason too many of your problems are getting you down instead of you living above them!

"Well," you say, "at least I'll go to heaven."

That's great, but I ask you, "What if you are delayed a few or many years? What if you don't go to heaven right away? Then you've got to face the mountains of life . . . the needs and problems that come to you in the now."

I doubt if you ever have one day without problems. I have a feeling that even now you have problems you cannot handle and there's some real doubt in your mind about them ever getting solved. As far as you are concerned about the problem, you wish you were in heaven right now. But I'm telling you that a lot of those problems can be solved in the NOW. When I say IN THE NOW, I mean they can start being solved now. Most problems don't get solved in a second, most of them get solved over a period of time.

Somehow if I just know mine are going to get solved I

start feeling better. Whether it's going to get solved today or not, or solved next month or even a year from now, that's better than having no hope at all. I believe the greatest problem you can have is to reach a place where you lose hope . . . where you think things are never going to change. It's terrible to lose hope.

I'm talking to you now about putting in a seed of faith and putting it in your Source. And your Source is the Lord Jesus Christ.

What is the source a farmer puts his seed in? It is the earth, isn't it? It is the ground. Unless God had put ground or earth here for the farmer to plow and to sow seed in, he could never reap a harvest. You can't sow seed in thin air. But God putting the earth as a source is not enough. It's like the man who had a beautiful productive farm. A man walked by and said, "My, isn't it wonderful what God has done here."

The farmer said, "That's right, but you should have seen this place when God had it by himself." What he meant was, "Sure, God has given me this farm. This earth is God's. But I've plowed it and I've sown it and I've built it and harvested it. I'm working on this farm just as the Lord intended. And it's God and me." That makes sense to me because you don't get something for nothing. You've got to do your part, then God can do His. God says you've got to give in order to receive:

> *Give, and it shall be given unto you; good measure, pressed down, and shaken together, and running over, shall men give into your bosom* (Luke 6:38).

Men shall even give to you . . . "into your bosom." This means men will be influenced to give to you. (*Men* means male and female.) It means people will be influenced to give to you and to give to you far more than you have given. That is, you receive in a multiplied form—"good measure, shaken together, and even running over." Jesus said it and it's true.

Jesus also said:

> *For with what measure you give, it shall be measured to you again.*

Whatever you give, that's what you are going to receive. That will be the measure of your receiving, except it will be multiplied when it comes back to you.

WITH WHAT MEASURE YOU GIVE . . .

Let me tell you a story about a farmer and a baker who were close friends. The baker bought his butter from the farmer and the farmer bought his bread from the baker. One day the baker became upset with the farmer because he weighed the butter and found that the package of butter did not weigh a pound. So he said, "Good friend farmer, you are cheating me on my butter. I'm getting less than a pound when I buy it from you."

"Oh, no," the farmer said to his baker friend, "I'm your friend. I would never do you that way. It's a pound."

He said, "It's not."

And the farmer said, "Well, I'm sure that's not true."

When they could not settle it the baker took his friend farmer to court. The judge said to the farmer, "Why are you shortchanging your friend, the baker? Why are you selling him a pound of butter that weighs less than a pound?"

He said, "Judge, I'm selling him butter in pound lots."

"How do you know it weighs a pound?"

"Well," he said, "I just know."

"Well, how do you determine this?"

He said, "I weigh it on a big old pair of scales in my

barn. I admit that the scales are big and usually don't weigh really tiny things on it, but it's the best I've got. I'm very honest."

"Well," the judge said, "it's short."

"Well," the farmer said, "I don't just stop by weighing the butter on my old scales. Each week I go to the store and buy a pound loaf of the bread friend baker sells. And I always measure my butter according to the pound weight of his bread."

The judge dismissed the case.

With what measure you give it shall be measured back to you. That's what our Lord said. If you want to be loved, you have to love first. If you want to be given to . . . you must give first.

ONLY WHAT YOU GIVE CAN BE MULTIPLIED

There are some things you can't buy. If you had all the money in the world you couldn't buy someone's love . . . you couldn't buy perfect health. There are many things that you can't buy, you have to get them by loving . . . you get them by giving. You get them by putting seed in first. It's more blessed (productive) to give than it is to receive because only what you give is multiplied back—never what you receive.

For example, say that I'm a wheat farmer and someone gives me a hundred bushels of wheat. If I put the hundred bushels of wheat in my barn, does it multiply? No. Suppose I take that hundred bushels of wheat and I plant it. Does it multiply? Yes. Our Lord is saying, *what people give you that you keep will not multiply.* It is more productive to give than to receive (Acts 20:35). It is what you give that's multiplied back, not what you receive and keep. That's why Jesus says that if you have faith to put a seed in and you do it first, you then can speak to the mountains of problems you face. The reason this is so is because if you put the seed in FIRST you know the eternal law of seed-time and harvest, given by God way back in Genesis 8:22 and carried on through the New Testament into the NOW, is working for you. Christ's words are true, "Give, and it shall be given unto you."

I have a friend who is 70 years old. He is a wonderful giver. But something bad happened in his life and he broke down and cried. He said, "Oral, I have put the seed in. For years I've practiced Seed-Faith just like you said. I've made a pattern of giving. I give of my money. I give of my time. I'm concerned about people."

The tears were running down his cheeks. As he cried, I cried too. I knew it was the truth. Yet this thing was so bad that he couldn't handle it. It was a mountain he could not remove from his life. In a way, I was embarrassed because I'd influenced his life and now it looked like what I had preached was false. All I could say to him was, "Dear, dear friend, what I've told you is the truth. What you've done is right. You have practiced the eternal law of our Lord. God is going to help you."

He said, "Well, He hasn't."

I said, "Have you ever thought of the Scripture that says:

> *Let us not be weary in well doing: for in due season we shall reap, if we faint not* (Galatians 6:9)?

This means you will reap if you don't get discouraged!"

He said, "No, I hadn't thought of that."

I said, "Let me give you an example. There is a *due season* when you harvest. If you plant wheat or corn you don't go out to gather in the harvest until the *due season.* Another example: If you agree with a man to work for him for two weeks and then you will be paid . . . there is a due season for your pay. You work the two weeks *first* THEN you get paid. That is your *due season.*"

"Well," he said, "*when* is my due season?"

I said, "I cannot tell you. Only God, our Source, knows. I wish I could tell you." We were like two little children sitting there crying. He hurt and I hurt. Looks like everything I've preached is false. I said, "All I can tell you is two things: one, keep on sowing the seed and two, know in your heart there's going to be a due season. Expect a miracle."

"Oh," he said, "I've expected the miracle."

But I said, "*Keep on* expecting the miracle. Don't give up . . . don't get weary in well-doing . . . don't throw it all away . . . don't stop now."

I didn't know if I had any effect on him in that moment because he sounded quite disappointed, even bitter. I could understand that because I've been bitter too. I've almost said, "God, You don't even know who I am. You don't care whether I live or die." But one thing is true, God is going to do what He says but He's going to do it at His time. And He's going to do it in His way. That's why you've got to learn His way.

This happened several months ago. Just a short time later I talked to my friend John again and he was so excited and thrilled. I said, "What's happened?"

To sum it all up what he really said was, "MY due season is beginning to come. Oral, what I needed in my own body is starting to happen." He was excited and in essence he said, "Man, am I going to keep on planting seed in the future!" He saw the value of staying a plant-ER.

I tell you, when you sow seed—seed of your concern, seed of your money, seed of your time, there's going to be a due season for it. You've got to expect it. Look for it. But if you get too discouraged you won't recognize the harvest when it comes. Discouraged people don't see miracles coming. You've got to *look up* to see them. Look up!

Have you ever heard the phrase:

IT JUST CAME TO ME OUT OF THE BLUE

Did you ever have anything come to you that just seemed to COME OUT OF THE BLUE? I mean, you couldn't explain it? Well, I believe that what seemed to "come out of the blue" was really the harvest from seed that you had planted sometime before. In other words, your due season had arrived. God had just given you the harvest of your seed-sowing in a different way from what you had been expecting.

Did you know that you seldom get anything from God exactly the way you thought you wanted it? His ways are not our ways. I know that God seldom gives me exactly what I ask for. Seldom does He give it to me WHEN I want it because that would have been yesterday. Friend, if you don't think I can diagram it out for God, you ought to be around me sometime. I can tell Him exactly how to run matters—but am I glad He sticks to His method rather than mine! Because His *way* and *time* of doing it is always better than mine.

I want to encourage you to keep putting the seed in. Try to think about the seed and not the mountain. TRY! I know it's hard. Try to have the courage to put a seed in rather than just begging God to move the mountain.

Honestly, friend, if you get the seed of faith in, God's going to work through that seed and He will move the mountain. If it's ever going to be moved, God will have to move it. You will never move it. There's no way you can move it. If your problems are going to be solved, there's going to have to be Somebody bigger than you to solve them. And He's not necessarily going to use your method. It may just come out of the blue. I don't mean to overemphasize that but I can't think of another statement that fits so well. Because even though we say it came out of the blue, that's not what we mean. We mean that Somebody out there was thinking about us. We mean that God remembered us.

I know that my God is so concerned about you. I know He wants to supply your needs. Perhaps you don't know what Seed-Faith is. You may give a little here and a little there but you haven't formed a pattern of giving. And of giving as a SEED. Now one thing I have tried to do, and I recommend it to you, is to form a pattern of giving and make it the forward thrust of your life. Before I ask for anything from God, I give something. I gave something before we built Oral Roberts University. My wife and I gave every dollar in the world we had saved. We went broke in one day. The money we gave alone couldn't build the school but it was a seed and we put it in. I'm telling you the truth. I don't own anything. I'm on a salary and I'm not bragging about it or complaining. I'm telling the truth. I put some seed in and God gave the harvest. I've tried to form a pattern. Now sometimes I get busy or worried about something and forget who my Source is. Every time I forget who my Source is, I fail. Every time I fail to put a seed in and I expect God to give me a miracle, it never, never, never, never comes. Every time after I put the seed in and I demand to receive the harvest right now, nine times out of ten God doesn't give it then. He makes me wait. "Wait on the Lord" (Proverbs 20:22). Here's the nice thing about that. The nice thing about becoming a SOW-ER, or to translate that—to become a follower of Christ, not only to put in a few seeds once in a while but to constantly put seed in—is that the harvest becomes cumulative . . . CUMULATIVE! That is:

> GOD BUILDS A PERSONAL STOREHOUSE FOR THE GIVER IN WHICH HE STORES UP THE MIRACLES THAT WE WILL NEED IN EACH OF OUR DUE SEASONS . . . THAT IS THE CUMULATIVE EFFECT!

I believe God has a personal storehouse in which He stores all of Oral Roberts' miracles, and all of your miracles —God holds our miracles for His due season. So those moments when I need a miracle . . . when you need a miracle . . . it seems to come to us out of the blue. It seems that our miracle has our name on it.

For example, if I had to depend on God to supply all the needs of Oral Roberts University, the television and radio ministry, and this total ministry I couldn't do it. I couldn't have that kind of faith. It's too big of a mountain. But I've been working on it for years. I've been sowing the seed and it's *cumulative.* Things that people have been doing, and said they were going to do from time to time, are being done. And it comes in and it accumulates. Those miracles begin to happen. The various due seasons come. He keeps opening my personal storehouse in which He has stored up the miracles that I need in each of my due seasons. The cumulative effect is constantly taking effect. I've learned that is God's pattern with me . . . if I have been constantly planting seed.

Now let's take you. Say that you have not been a constant planter of seed—a sow-ER. You've not formed a pattern of being a seed planter but you want to start. I want to encourage you not only to start but to do it constantly and *make it an attitude of your life.* I encourage you to think of it as a joyous thing. Not as a debt you owe, but as a seed you sow.

GIVE, NOT AS A DEBT YOU OWE BUT AS A SEED YOU SOW

Friend, don't ever say, "I owe this to God." Please don't ever say it. You don't mean it wrong but it's wrong to say it. Christ has paid the debt. You are saying that you can pay it, but you can't. Christ suffered on the cross and rose from the dead. He paid the price. If you had a million dollars and you walked up and said, "Here it is, God," you couldn't pay Him for what Christ has done for you. You don't owe it because He's paid all you owe. Christ has paid all I owe.

You say, "But I've got something that I should give to the Lord." That's true, but think of it as a seed you sow—not as something you owe. It's through that seed that God is going to help people and He's going to multiply it back to you. That's how He's going to meet your needs. That's His way of doing things. (Remember I said, learn God's way of doing things.) Every word I've said is the truth of God. It is the Bible. If you will take it and you will do it, I not only promise you—I guarantee you—that God is going to give you miracles.

THE SECRET OF LIFE IS IN EXPECTING MIRACLES.

You expect the miracles from the seed of faith that you put in. You expect miracles when you give first. And what do you give? Yourself. You give yourself to Jesus.

GIVE GOD YOUR BEST THEN ASK HIM FOR HIS BEST . . . THE GREATER THE SACRIFICE, THE GREATER THE BLESSING

To me, that's what it is to be a follower of Christ. That's what it is to take up your cross daily and follow Him. That's what it means to deny yourself because your self doesn't want to give. Your self wants only to receive. Am I right? You've got to turn that around, and so have I.

If you miss everything else I say in this chapter I want you to remember this: You've got to give God seed . . . you've got to give Him something to work miracles with. You may say, "Well, I thought God was merciful." Yes, God is merciful but He has laws that He intends for you to live by. And you've got to keep His laws . . . and you've got to do it consistently day by day–DAILY. The cross has to be carried daily. You've got to become a disciple. Giving has to become a part of you. You can start and God will bless you. Then you can keep on doing it all the days of your life and He will bless you and bless you and bless you.

It's hard to love and to give. But you cannot love without giving and you cannot give without loving. It's not always easy to be concerned about someone else and their needs– we think the most about our own concerns and problems. It just goes against the grain, doesn't it, to be concerned about others? That's why the MAN said, in essence, "If you want to be My disciple, take up your CROSS DAILY . . . that is, DENY yourself."

I tell you it is the hardest thing in the world to be a disciple. It's hard enough to repent and be converted. It takes a lot of honesty and courage to admit that you are a sinner . . . to repent and ask God to save you. But it's a lot harder to do it *every* day. Day after day after day. It's hard to walk up and tell a fellow, "I am wrong." It's much easier to say, "You are wrong." But Seed-Faith living is becoming a disciple of our Lord. It's beginning with our faith and MAKING IT INTO SOMETHING.

Jesus said:

> If ye have faith as a grain of mustard seed . . .

Now Jesus didn't say to "have faith" only, He said to have faith AS a grain of seed that you plant . . . that is, to make your faith something that you give . . . something that you give FIRST.

This is the Seed-Faith principle. This is the message of the gospel. It is the Good News . . .

YOU PUT SOMETHING OF YOURSELF IN AS SEED–
no matter how small you feel,
or how big your need is,
or how difficult your problem is,
or how severe the shortages are in your life–
YOU START GIVING OF YOUR TOTAL SELF.
GOD'S LAW OF THE HARVEST DOES THE REST.
IT REPRODUCES A MIRACULOUS HARVEST IN YOUR LIFE. IT MOVES THAT MOUNTAIN– THOSE MOUNTANS. IT NEVER FAILS BECAUSE JESUS SAID IT!

I believe it and I know it.

2

How You Can Get Into An Atmosphere That Attracts The Miracles Of God

DO YOU HAVE trouble believing in miracles? Well, I can understand that because there was a time in my life that I wouldn't have recognized a miracle if I met it coming down the road. I mean, it was something so far beyond what I could grasp. God was just a blur in my mind. But one day something dawned in my mind about God. I had a need that couldn't be met by myself, though I tried so hard. That need could not be met by my parents or by anybody in the world. It took God. It took a miracle! And that's when I began to open up and understand about miracles. A miracle happened to me! That's why I believe that you and I can live in a rhythm of miracles. Miracles CAN happen to you.

In Luke 5 is a powerful story about our Lord and the disciples. It's the story of empty nets, of frustrated fishermen who have worked hard but have nothing to show for their labor. It's the story of you and me today . . . of paychecks that just can't stretch to meet all our needs . . . of businesses that don't make enough profit to pay the bills. But it's the story of hope, too—a story of God's unlimited miracle supply.

You know, when Jesus came on the scene things changed!!! He showed people how to get into a rhythm of faith, into an atmosphere of miracles that changed the situation. I mean,

IT CHANGED THINGS. What was the thing that needed changing in this situation? Well, these men were commercial fishermen; that's the way they made their living.

Why would God be concerned about fishermen and empty nets?

Why should God care about your financial needs?

Why should God be concerned about the way you make your living? Because He's concerned about the total man. God is concerned about a man—his wife, his children, everything that his family does. He's concerned about the food you eat, the clothes you wear, the car you drive, the house you live in, your career or job or business. He's concerned about you and He's involved with you.

GOD IS INVOLVED WITH EACH OF US

Now on this occasion Jesus came down to the Sea of Galilee and a tremendous crowd followed to hear Him preach . . . a crowd so large that He didn't have a place to stand where everybody could see and hear Him. So He looked over and saw three or four men by their empty boats. They were washing and working on their worn and empty nets. Jesus saw the crowd. But He also saw THEM—three or four individual men. That's the way Jesus Christ is.

In a crowd it's hard to think that anybody really notices you, let alone God. But here Jesus Christ is about to preach to thousands. Yet He looks over and sees three or four men battling with life's everyday problems—and Jesus sees the problem. He sees that they have faced futility, that the boat is empty. He sees that they are looking down and they feel bad. He sees that they are in need. So thinking of them, He says, "Lend Me your boat."

Now the boat wasn't full. There wasn't anything about the boat that really could help Jesus Christ as far as it being full of something. When He said, "Lend Me your boat," He was thinking of their need.

When you give something to God He doesn't want to keep it. He just wants to use it and multiply it and give it back. This is why I keep saying to myself:

> GIVE GOD YOUR BEST THEN ASK HIM FOR HIS BEST . . . THE GREATER THE SACRIFICE, THE GREATER THE BLESSING.

Well, right in the midst of a negative situation, in the middle of all their trouble, these fishermen loaned Jesus their boat. I mean they started giving . . . they started opening up. They had hit bottom, you might say. They didn't know where to turn. Then Jesus Christ approached them by asking them for something. He asked them to get involved with Him in the gospel—to start giving Him their best. And the best they had was their boat. That's the way they made their living. But they gave it and He used it, and when He finished preaching He turned right back to them and said, "Now, launch out into the deep and let down your nets for a catch."

And Peter said, "Well, now look, Lord, we've toiled all night and have taken nothing."

The fact of the matter is that the water of the Sea of Galilee is so crystal clear that you can't fish in the day because the fish see the nets. So you have to fish at night, particularly in the dark of the moon. So Peter was really saying, "Look, if you can't net fish at night, how can you net them in the day?" You see, Peter was going by his rules of life and not thinking of what God was saying.

Peter was thinking of the mountain, the mountain of impossibility of netting fish during the day rather than night. Peter was also thinking of the mountain of having to go back to the same sea where he had already failed only the previous night. What a big mountain that was to him. BUT JESUS

WAS THINKING OF THE SEED PETER HAD GIVEN HIM TO WORK WITH. JESUS KNEW WITH THAT SEED HE COULD MOVE THE MOUNTAIN AND GIVE THEM THE MIRACLE CATCH THEY NEEDED.

God wasn't concerned about the day or the night because He controls this world and all that's in it. So He decides whether or not the fish will strike the net—and when.

Jesus Christ saw that these fishermen could have a miracle. They had opened up. They had begun to give to Him. They had loaned Him their boat and now He's seeking to get them into a rhythm of faith or . . .

A PATTERN FOR MIRACLES

You see, your pattern of miracles follows your pattern of seed-sowing. Finally, after a lot of struggle, Peter said, "Nevertheless, at thy word I will let down the net . . ." Or in other words, Peter said, "Lord, because we put the seed in and You said to expect a miracle, we'll do it." When he did this he was transferring his thoughts to a new kind of idea . . . a new way of thinking . . . GOD IS MY SOURCE . . . Jesus is my Source.

In other words, Peter is saying, "This boat is not my Source . . .

not these nets,

not the sea,

not even the fish out there,

but this Man right here—Jesus Christ—He's the Source of my life. I've put the seed of faith in, NOW I'm expecting a miracle." *Peter is getting into a rhythm of faith—into an atmosphere that attracts miracles.*

My wife Evelyn tells a story about our little granddaughter Marcia that will shed some light on this subject. I want her to tell it to you like she told it to me recently when we were on a panel.

EVELYN: Well, when Marcia was a baby our daughter Rebecca created an *atmosphere* of sleep for her. She had a little music box that she hung on the side of the crib. And when she put Marcia in bed she'd turn this little music box on. When Marcia heard the music she knew it was time to go to sleep. She would just rub her eyes, curl up in a little tight ball, and pretty soon she was sound asleep.

Really, Oral, it's like when you and I used to travel so much . . . and still do. When we walked into a motel or hotel room there was just no atmosphere at all . . .

ORAL: That's the truth. Not like home, was it?

EVELYN: No. So I would unpack our suitcases, put some pictures of the grandchildren all around, take out the Bible and some books like MIRACLE OF SEED-FAITH and THE MIRACLE BOOK and lay them on the tables, and perhaps our "Expect a Miracle" plaque. Then it was "home." I felt like I'd created a "home" atmosphere.

ORAL: That's good, Evelyn.

Do you see what she is saying—there was an atmosphere created for our little granddaughter Marcia. When she heard the music she began to rub her eyes and expected to go to sleep. And in our motel room we would just surround ourselves with these things to create the kind of atmosphere we wanted to live in. In the same way, *you* can *create* an atmosphere of miracle living. That's what we are saying.

A NET-BREAKING, BOAT-SINKING LOAD!

Now I want you to see Jesus standing there in the boat. See the disciples launching out into the deep. They finally got into this rhythm and they are expecting . . . they are expecting. So they throw the net over and the God who created the fish said, "Strike that net, strike that net." And they hit it. I mean, they hit it and they filled it so full it began to break up. They pulled it into the boat and it was so heavy the boat began to sink. They got a net-breaking, boat-sinking load!

This is a total change from toiling all night and getting nothing and then suddenly having a net-breaking, boat-sinking load. I mean, they moved somewhere. This is what a miracle does. A miracle settles an issue. It gets the job done. It changes your life.

But you have to get into a rhythm, an atmosphere of miracles. And you do this by asking yourself, "Who is my source? What am I looking to or to whom am I looking?" Ultimately you've got to look to God as your Source of total supply.

> *But my God shall supply all your need according to his riches in glory by Christ Jesus* (Philippians 4: 19).

If you could memorize that verse, *really* commit it to memory . . . and put it down into your heart and make it a way of life, an attitude, it would turn your life around.

When you begin to think about your needs and you think about them long enough, you get low. Because you can't see any way to get them met. Sometimes you say, "If I could just get ONE need met, I'd be happy . . ." But the Bible goes beyond that. The Bible says, "My God shall supply ALL your need . . ."

Now I realize it takes trust. It takes faith to believe that. But the whole Bible is based on faith. Believing in God is based on faith. You have to go beyond the sense level of *sight, hearing, taste, smell,* and *feeling* on which you live on this earth in order to believe. You have to go down in your inner man and pull up that extra something God put there, and it's called faith.

You've got to BELIEVE this, "MY God . . . my God . . ." Not just God, but God who is *my* God. My personal God. God who is my personal Savior and Lord, the Lord of my life. It becomes a way of life when you say, "MY God." It personalizes God. It sensitizes your feelings toward God. It makes you very intimate and sensitive about God and toward God. Oh, it's so important to you and to me to grasp that . . . to know it as truth inside ourselves.

"For my God shall supply all your need . . ." How in the world can He do it? You can't see Him. Where is He? We are down here on a *sense* level. We hurt, we are struck at, needs pile up around us. Problems arise until we almost go out of our minds. On the level of our senses we *feel* all these things, including tasting, smelling, seeing and hearing. So you can ask, how can God supply all your need? He says, according to His riches in glory by Christ Jesus.

THERE IS A SOURCE OF POWER
FOR YOUR HUMAN NEEDS . . .
YOUR HUMAN PROBLEMS . . .
YOUR HUMAN LIMITATIONS . . .
AND THAT SOURCE OF POWER IS GOD

You have to fit into God. You have to get a personal relationship with God. Like me, there will be a time in your life when God just sort of DAWNS on you. And you begin to be conscious of Him, that He exists, that He is, and that He's a rewarder of them that earnestly seek Him (Hebrews 11:6). You have to know that God is good and that God will *always* be good . . . and that God loves YOU.

I know a doctor who is a great surgeon. He went into his operating room one day to relax a few minutes between operations. And he lay down on the operating table. Suddenly it dawned on him, "It's lonely in here." And he thought for a moment of all the people he had operated on . . . and about the feelings they must have had when they got into the operating room. He is a Christian and a strong believer in God as His Source, so he had a little sign painted on the ceiling above the operating table which read GOD LOVES YOU. He said he's had fantastic success with this. People will look up and read GOD LOVES YOU. And for many, it's a dawning of God.

You see, in the intimate details of your life God becomes your Source if you will only accept Him as the Source of your supply . . . if you will only enter into an atmosphere that attracts the miracles of God.

GOD CAN AND WILL MEET YOUR NEEDS . . .
GOD CAN AND WILL GIVE YOU A MIRACLE.

THE WIDOW'S MEAL BARREL

There's also a story in the Bible about a widow who made a Seed-Faith pact with God. This woman and her young son had only enough food for a day (1 Kings 17:8-16). There was a famine in the land. She had no one to turn to. Then God sends her a messenger and really gives her an opportunity to get her needs met.

Have you ever noticed that when you get a pain it's worse than anybody else's pain? Have you ever noticed that when you run out of money you feel worse than anybody that ever ran out of money? Have you ever gotten down spiritually and you didn't feel like getting up or going anywhere and you thought, I just feel worse than anybody in the world feels. I think we are all alike. It's not the *degree* of trouble we are in, it's how that degree affects us. AND THAT'S WHERE THIS WIDOW WAS WHEN GOD CAME DOWN TO MEET HER NEEDS.

The instrument of God the great Source was the prophet Elijah . . . and it happened that Elijah didn't have anything to eat either. (How do you like that? The instrument God may choose to help you may have needs too.)

When Elijah arrived he found the widow outside picking up sticks to make a fire and cook her last meal. And the first thing he said was, "Give me some water, please." Now Elijah was testing the widow when he asked her for a drink of water. He found she was willing to give it. Then he asked her for something to eat . . . and that stopped her cold. Giving Elijah a drink of water was one thing—giving him her last bit of food was something else. She had to admit that she had only enough to cook one meal for her son and herself. They were going to eat it and die.

Elijah said, "That's all right, you go ahead and cook it. But FIRST make a little cake for me—the servant of God—and then make one for yourself and your son."

GOD'S AREA AND MAN'S AREA

Now we get into the area of God. There's a line between man and God. On one side of the line is God. On the other side of the line is man. Man can just go so far, then he comes to the end. But when he crosses over into faith in God . . . then he gets over there where God can do something that he cannot do. That's the big difference. You get over into the realm of miracles. But you've got to do something *first.* You've got to open up and start giving, start loving, start relating. Jesus said, "Love the Lord thy God with all thy heart . . ." and then "Love thy neighbour as thyself" (Matthew 22:37, 39). You can talk all you want to but this is where it's at. This is loving God and loving people. This is *giving* and *loving.*

So Elijah was telling the widow this in so many words and then he said, "The Lord says that your food supply will not diminish. Go ahead and cook the last bit you've got and it will not diminish"—a miracle, yes. That put her on the spot.

Now she has to believe. She has to believe God. Or she has to doubt God. She can give God her best and then ask Him for His best, or she can say, "No."

When you give God your best; that is, when you give out of your great need, that's real giving. That's the kind God's going to send back. The giving that God's going to multiply back to meet your need is the kind that reaches down inside you . . .

> that smile when it hurts to smile . . .
> that loving when it hurts to love . . .
> that giving of funds when it hurts to give.

But you give it TO God. And God isn't going to keep it. He's just going to *use* it and *multiply* it and send it right back to you.

This reminds me of a Scripture that is sort of hidden away in the New Testament. I think it's just fabulous. It's found in Mark 11. Do you remember the story of Palm Sunday? Jesus rides a donkey right down the main streets of Jerusalem and the people shout "Hosannah to the Lord," and put palm branches in the streets before Him. But do you remember that Jesus had to borrow the donkey He rode? One of the translators of this verse says it this way:

> *He* (Jesus) *sent off two of his disciples with these instructions, "Go into the village just ahead of you and as soon as you enter it you will find a tethered colt on which no one has yet ridden. Untie it, and bring it here. If anybody asks you, 'Why are you doing this?' just say, 'The Master needs him, and will send him back immediately' "*
> (Mark 11:1-3, Phillips translation).

Now Jesus knew there was a certain man in Jerusalem who

had a donkey and He needed him. And I imagine that this thought went through our Lord's mind, if I send My disciples over there and ask him for this donkey, this man will be wondering if he will ever get him back.

And that's exactly what goes through our mind—if we'll be honest about it—when we feel God wants something from us. What's going to happen to it?? To me?? And a great many people don't give because they think it will diminish them and they will have less than they had before they gave. So Jesus said, in effect, "You tell this man that the Master needs his donkey but I'll send him right back."

Have you ever thought about what happened to that donkey? Well, I know one thing—that donkey didn't come back in the same spirit that he was brought to Jesus because he had never been ridden by the Lord. The King of kings had never been astride him. Before, this was just a plain old donkey. I mean really plain. But after Jesus rode on this donkey in the triumphal entry into Jerusalem and then sent the donkey right back, he became a special donkey. He was now a kingly donkey. This was a donkey that had carried majesty, divinity, the Son of God. He had been an instrument of the Lord of lords.

YOU ARE NEVER DIMINISHED WHEN YOU GIVE TO GOD

Have you ever thought about what happens when you give to God by your love . . . when you relate to people and give out of yourself . . . I mean, you let the goodness of God come out of you in your talents and your time and your concern and your money and whatever you have that you give to God?

God says to you, "I need that, not to keep but to use and bless and multiply and send it right back. And never will it be the same again." When you give something to God and He returns it, it will never be the same again—it will not be diminished but rather, multiplied . . . because God has touched it.

Well, the widow of Zarephath made the decision to give God her best. There was something about Elijah, God's instrument, that created an atmosphere for believing in miracles—and it would certainly take a miracle to meet her needs. So she gave out of her want and began to EXPECT A MIRACLE. She gave the *first* cake to Elijah and when she began to make a second cake she discovered that her supply had not been diminished. She cooked for herself and her son and it wasn't diminished. So they just kept on—day after day after day after day. She kept cooking for herself and her son and it still wasn't diminished. Here was the miracle of the meal barrel (1 Kings 17:14-16). Day after day after day after day after day THE MIRACLES KEPT ON COMING.

You don't have to stop with one miracle, because you need more than one miracle. You need God your Source who is an unending Source of miracles. You can translate God any way you want to but . . .

GOD IS AN UNENDING SOURCE OF MIRACLES FOR YOUR LIFE

Today you can enter into a rhythm of miracles, into a Seed-Faith pact with God, in which you make Him the Source of your total supply, you start giving of your total being as a seed you plant, and you start expecting His miracles. If you will say, "Yes, God, I'll give You my best and then I'll ask You for Your best," and really start doing it you will begin getting needs met. You will begin having miracles. And what is even more important, you will continue to have them.

3

How You Can Be At Peace With Yourself Over Personal Guilt

In a recent issue of the Tulsa Tribune, which is owned and edited by my good friend, Jenkin Lloyd Jones, also a nationally known syndicated writer, he wrote an article entitled *The Fading Alibi.* In it he quoted Dr. Karl Menninger, the famous psychiatrist who has just published a new book, *Whatever Became of Sin.* Mr. Jones says:

> The concept of sin has been out of fashion too long. We have been deep in the business of inventing tortured alibis for human misbehavior and the result has been a growing chaos in our society and a danger to our citizens.
>
> "There is sin," writes Dr. Menninger, "which cannot be subsumed under verbal artifacts such as disease, delinquency, deviancy. There is immorality. There is unethical behavior. There is wrongdoing."
>
> That's why a . . . man must have a sense of sin. He must be uncomfortable with his tendencies toward evil and irresponsibility. . . . It has been a long time since Billy Sunday ordered his weeping tent congregations to "hit the sawdust trail." It was

> a pretty corny . . . way to salvation. But recently we have been on a six-lane, limited access, superhighway to hell.
>
> And for our own personal happiness and peace of mind the eminent Dr. Menninger suggests we get off at the next exit.

I think that's one of the most powerful statements said in the now to you and me of our generation.

In Paul's writing is the statement about our Lord Jesus:

> *This is a faithful saying, and worthy of all acceptation, that Christ Jesus came into the world to save sinners; of whom I am chief* (1 Timothy 1:15).

Jesus Christ always told the truth. When He began His public ministry, He talked about the good news of the gospel. He went around opening doors for people and showing them the better life. But as He neared the end of His life, the last five or six months, there was a strange change in the look on His face and the sound of His voice and the words of His mouth. He began to talk about the consequences of rejecting God, the consequences of sin, and what's going to happen to a person who remains a sin-NER. It's always Jesus' method to start with the good things, to hold out the promises of life, but if they're ignored or rejected, then He tells the truth about the consequences of such sin. Here's the truth that Jesus Christ tells to you and me.

FIRST, ALL SIN WILL BE PUNISHED

All sin will be punished unless it's repented of and forgiven of God. Now the lines are drawn for that, not only in the published laws of the Bible, the Word of God, but in the moral and physical laws of this universe. It's an accepted scientific fact that nature will rise up and punish you if you break its laws. Even in our everyday life, if you run a red light you may get by the first time or the second or even the third time. But if you keep running red lights you are going to hurt someone, or get hurt. You are going to kill somebody, or get killed. Those who build the spaceships to the moon tell us that unless they obey the laws of nature in an exact way, that the laws of nature will rise up and punish them. The spaceship will explode. If the astronaut tries to breathe the atmosphere of the moon without the proper oxygen equipment it will destroy him because it is poisonous. So the laws of both the Bible and the universe tell us that all sin will be punished.

SECOND, THE PUNISHMENT FOR SIN WILL BE JUST

It will be just because of the Man who is the judge. There will be no bribery. There will be no political influence because He will go by the eternal laws of God.

Now consider who He is. Jesus Christ is the Man who came down to earth and became a man. He was tempted in all points like you and I are (Hebrew 4:15).

If you've ever been tempted, and surely you are every day, just remember that Christ faced that same temptation, only more so because the devil wanted to destroy Him more than anyone else. If you've ever had the feeling of lust, remember that the devil tempted our Lord with lust even more so. If you've had the urge of anger to the extent of killing, remember that the devil brought that same temptation to our Lord. When it was all over, Jesus had faced every sin, every temptation. He had faced them as a mere human being, and He did it without yielding to one temptation. He showed us that it could be done. Then as God He went to the cross to die and become the Savior. He said, in essence, "I went through it and did it." This is why *it's so important to know Jesus and follow Him because He's the only one qualified to take you through life.* He became our Savior, but at the judgment He is no longer our Savior. He becomes our judge.

There is a true story about two brothers that moves me deeply. One was always getting into trouble. The other had a great desire to make something of himself and to do the things that are uplifting. Still, he loved his brother who was always getting into trouble, so he always helped him out. Then one day the wayward brother made a fatal mistake. He decided, "No matter what kind of mess I get into my brother will get me out of it." While he was so busy getting into trouble it escaped him that this brother went on to become a judge. The next time he broke the law they brought him into court, but he wasn't worried. He said, "It's OK. It'll be all right. I've got a brother who will get me out." The officials told him to stand as the judge came in. When he looked up, there was his brother, except now he had on the robe of the judge. For a long time the brothers looked at each other in astonished silence. It was a high moment of recognition. As the court proceeded, the wayward brother kept trying to signal the judge, "Look, I'm your brother. You've always helped me. You've always got me out of trouble. I'm your brother." Finally the judge made an open statement that although the offender was his brother, he had to go by the law. The court found his brother guilty and the judge, in spite of his emotions, had to pass sentence on him. As the brother was led away he was heard to say, "But you're my brother."

And the judge, with the tears streaming down his cheeks, said, "Yes, yesterday I was your brother but today I am your judge."

TODAY JESUS CHRIST IS YOUR SAVIOR BUT TOMORROW HE WILL BE YOUR JUDGE

His judgment will be eminently fair and just. Your final judgment will not be because you've committed sin, but because you remained a sin-NER. The final judgment of you, I repeat, will not be because you've sinned, but because you remain a sin-NER. You will be judged and you will be found guilty because in your heart you've decided to sin forever; because in your heart you have formed a life pattern, a way of life, a life that has a tendency toward sin, a direction toward wrong. You will carry this with you into death and into the judgment. You will be judged, not for one sin but for being a sin-NER.

For example, the act of fornication between two unmarried people can be forgiven. Even two or three times. But after awhile that person becomes a fornicator. There's a difference in committing an act of fornication and becoming a fornicat-OR, so that it becomes a way of life. It becomes a sin that is a way of life—a fornicat-OR. It is the same with adultery. An act of adultery can be forgiven. But when one lives in adult-ERY that means he's an adulterer. That is, he has not only committed sin, he's now a sin-NER. The Bible says in 1 Corinthians 6:9 that no fornicat*or* or adulter*er* or li*ar* shall have any part in the kingdom of God. It also says:

> *All liars shall have their part in the lake which burneth with fire* . . . (Revelations 21:8).

One can tell a lie and be forgiven but if he becomes a li*ar*, that is, if it becomes a way of life, a life-style, he becomes a sin-NER.

In medieval times there was a very famous blacksmith

who was known for chain-making. He made outstanding chains. One day an army invaded the town and captured the people, including him. They shackled them in irons and carried them away. This particular man, the blacksmith, was thrown into a dungeon and shackled with heavy chains. But he wasn't worried because he knew chains. He knew that in the average chain there's always one link that's weak, and that if you find the weak link and touch it at a certain point in a certain way it will snap. He was anxious for the guards to leave him. The moment they did he swiftly picked up the chain that bound him and began to examine it link by link to find the weak link. All of a sudden he let out a cry of pain. He sank to the floor in agony, for he had found his own personal mark upon the chain and realized he himself had made that chain. He knew he had never made a chain with a weak link. He knew he could not break it. Lying there on the floor he let out a bloodcurdling scream, "I will never get out!"

You say, "Oral Roberts, are you saying to me that through the decisions and choices of my life I'm forging a chain, link by link, on which is my personal life's mark? That there are no weak links in it, or that I cannot break any of those links?"

Friend, I'm not saying that. Christ is saying that. That whatsoever you sow, for bad or for good, it will be multiplied back to you. This is why Seed-Faith living is so important. Seed-Faith is the eternal answer. When you make God your Source and you're always giving and sowing *good* seed, then you can expect to reap God's goodness and mercy. God's eternal law of sowing and reaping is infallible. It's the eternal law. It will never fail. Anyplace . . . anytime . . . anywhere . . . it'll work for *any* human being.

But we must say, on the other hand, the seeds of sin are the same. They work the same . . . but with the opposite results. And there's no weak link. Without Jesus Christ—who went to the cross to take your place, to break the chain of sin you are forging in your life—you will never find the weak link and get free. You will never be free of the sins of your past . . . of the guilt that gnaws at your insides . . . you can never be at peace with yourself.

One man, an intellectual, had difficulty believing that a good God would ever send a man to judgment and ultimately to hell. He went to a great Christian theologian to discuss it. Patiently the Christian minister took him through the Bible and showed him the published moral law of God. Then he led him through the paths of the universal laws of nature and showed him that punishment is always sure and just. Reluctantly the great man accepted the fact that there is punishment for sin, that there is a hell. He said with great anguish of spirit to the minister, "I would give everything I have if I could change it."

The minister's face lighted up and he said, "That's just the point. God has already given everything. He gave His Son Jesus Christ to die on the cross, to break the chains, to forgive the sins that are repented of, to change your life-style, to break the pattern, to forgive and to say 'Go, and sin no more.' "

Friend, after you have repented and been forgiven you may stumble again, but through Christ your life-style is changed. The direction of your life now is toward God. Remember what the Bible says, "This is a faithful saying . . . that Christ Jesus came into the world to save sinners . . ." (1 Timothy 1:15). I believe that you can be saved through Christ . . . not only saved in the NOW but SAVED FOREVER. Not only can you have your sins forgiven today, but you can be changed from being a sinner. That is, your nature can be changed now and forever. The Christ who is *now* our Lord will be your Savior forevermore.

And now, would you be kind enough to join me in a prayer. It's a prayer I pray for myself. As Paul says, I'm the chief of sinners. Every one of us needs salvation, we need Christ. The sense of sin floods our spirit and we know that we need God. Let's pray.

Father, in the name of Your Son Jesus Christ who went to the cross and suffered our punishment and who can free us now from the burden and penalty of sin, we ask for forgiveness and salvation.

And, dear friend, I pray for you. I pray that in your heart you will open up to God. I pray you will release yourself to Him and truly repent, change your mind, and ask Christ to change the pattern of your being and to give you a new life. I pray you will live in His will forever and ever. I pray that a great healing will come to you in soul and body. Through Christ I pray and I believe and I expect a miracle. Amen and amen.

4

How To Build A Happy Home

RECENTLY I WAS ON THE WEST COAST and someone handed me an underground newspaper that was published by militant students. In the want ad section I read ads like this:

> *Come home, all is forgiven. Come home,*
> *John, you won't have to cut your hair.*
> *Come home, come home, Ann. We love you.*
> *You can attend church wherever you wish.*
> *Only come home, everything is forgiven.*

Let me tell you a story which I think illustrates what we are going through today. There was a family sitting at dinner and all of a sudden the little four-year-old son got up, stood on his chair, and shouted, "PASS THE BUTTER!!!"

His mother said, "Son, get down out of that chair!! Go to your room! You are not going to have any dinner tonight until you learn some manners!"

"But . . . but, Mother," the boy cried.

"No 'buts' about it, go to your room!"

So in tears the little boy went to his room.

Later that evening the father said to the family, "Come into the living room. You didn't know it but I made a recording of our conversation at dinner. I've been wanting to do this for a long time to catch us as we really are, and I want us all to listen." When he turned on the recorder there was the usual chatter. You know, "pass this" and "pass that" and "how are you?" and "what happened to you today?" Then there was a wee little voice that said, "Please, pass the butter." A little later the same voice, a little louder, said, "*Please*, pass the butter." After a while, the voice said again, "Will *somebody* please pass me the butter?"

Then all of a sudden, "PASS THE BUTTER!"

This story makes me wonder . . .

IS ANYBODY LISTENING??

I don't know if we parents are listening to our sons and daughters. They've been trying to get our attention. They've been trying to reach us.

On the other hand, some young people aren't listening either.

My wife used to be a schoolteacher and she tells this story. I get such a bang out of it. It happened with a schoolteacher away up in the mountains last winter. She was up there where it was snowing and she had to help the children with their wraps and their overshoes. There was this one little boy she was helping. She got down on her knees and she huffed and she puffed and she finally got his overshoes on. She stood up and the little boy said, "They're not mine." So she got down and she pulled and tugged and finally got them off and said, "OK, now?"

He looked up and said, "They're my sister's but she said I could wear them."

So the teacher got back down and she worked and she pulled and got them back on. Then the little boy looked up and said, "My mittens are down there inside them."

The situation with some of our youth today is like another

little boy I heard of. His grandfather was taking care of him. He fed him, rocked him, and nothing seemed to please him. Finally the young lad said, "Granddad, get up and walk me around and see if that's what I want."

You see where we are? We are messing around with our lives, with the lives of our children, with the lives of our loved ones, with something that's more precious than gold. We are not all listening and we are not all making up our minds. We are not concentrating upon the real issue.

The problem is not a generation gap, it's not an age gap, it's not an educational gap. It's not even a political gap. It is a spiritual gap.

I've talked to thousands of young people. I hear from thousands of young people. We have hundreds of them on the Oral Roberts University campus and I know many of them by their first names. I have dealt with hippies, militants, nonmilitants and all kinds of people in America. I've dealt with all races—here in America and overseas—the black, white, red, yellow, brown, and shades in between. Every time I've met a young person who is turned on to God, who is spiritual in his thinking and believes that God is the Source of his life and supply, there is no gap at all between us. I can talk to any young person like this. But I can talk to the other side too. (I have seen older people and young people sit down and have a fascinating conversation . . . talking about ideas and solving their problems. I've seen grandparents and teen-agers do it.)

Recently two high school seniors from Georgia hitchhiked all the way to where we were telecasting just to meet us. They said, "Mr. Roberts, we've been watching you on television. Here are our problems. We've been on drugs and things like that. We've got to have a talk with you." So we sat down and talked and then we prayed together. Later the young people on our telecast—the World Action Singers who are all ORU students—led those two seniors to Christ. Now they are turned on to God.

What I am saying is, the real problem is a *spiritual* gap. Once we understand that and begin with God, who is the Answer and the Source, everything has a chance to work out.

Now let me ask some questions of you as a parent and then I'll get around to the young people. If you are a parent, a father, mother, grandfather, or grandmother, or if you have someone under your care who is young, do you talk about God in your everyday life as naturally as you do when you are in church?

IS YOUR LIFE WITH GOD THE SAME AT HOME AS IT IS AT CHURCH?

Or do you have a sort of put-on kind of life that you live in a church service which you drop off when you get back home and it's not natural with you thereafter? Our children spot this and they call that hypocrisy . . . they call us phonies. What do you call it?

Well, you may say, "I can't act at home like I do at church." It's true you can't act the same way in methods such as sitting in a church pew and things like that, but in your heart you can. If you really love God, you love God wherever you are.

So I ask you: Do you use obscene language? Do you drink? Do you smoke? Do you gamble? Do you lie? Do you cheat? Do you commit adultery? Do you lust? What kind of pattern are you setting for your child? He sees everything you do.

What does the Bible mean to you? Do you make remarks that the Bible is for some other age? Or do you try to relate the Bible to the now of your experience?

DO YOU LOVE YOUR CHILD? DID YOU WANT HIM?

You know, a lot of parents don't want their children. Some mothers are turned off. Some fathers are so busy in their business they really don't want to bother with their children. And the children spot this kind of attitude. And it has a powerful, negative effect upon them. On the other hand, if you really want and love your children . . . and let them know that they are loved, this has a powerful effect for the GOOD.

YOUNG PEOPLE, DO YOU FLEE YOUTHFUL LUST?

Now, young person, let me ask you: Have you considered what the Bible says to you?

> *Remember now thy Creator in the days of thy youth* (Ecclesiastes 12:1).

The Bible also says:

> *Flee also youthful lusts* . . . (2 Timothy 2:22).

Are you fleeing youthful lusts? What do I see today? I see thousands of young people destroying themselves, abusing their bodies. The Bible says:

> *Know ye not that your body is the temple of the Holy Ghost* . . .

When you take your body—that beautiful body—and fill it with smoke, drugs, liquor, lust, or fornication, you are desecrating something really precious. Not only are you destroying your soul but you are destroying your body and that body is the temple of God.

> . . . *and ye are not your own? For ye are bought with*

a price: therefore glorify God in your body, and in your spirit, which are God's (1 Corinthians 6:19, 20).

DO YOU HONOR YOUR PARENTS?

You may disagree with your parents and it is normal that you will once in a while. You may learn some things that your parents don't know . . . or that you think they don't know. But when you disagree with your parents, do you love them? Do you honor and respect them? How long has it been since you spoke a kind word or wrote a letter or came home and put your arms around your parents and said, "I appreciate you and I love you"?

The Bible says:

God so loved . . . (John 3:16).

GOD SO LOVED . . . when we consider what God's love is . . . when we can let God express His love through us . . . when we can relate it to ourselves . . . to the relationships we have with our loved ones . . . then we can love our mother . . . we can love our father. Parent, you can love your children.

You know, our human love is a very precise thing. We are careful how we give it. We give it to some. We withhold it from others. We draw a dividing line between the two types of people: those we like and those we dislike . . . those whom we love and those whom we hate. I dislike using that word *hate* but sometimes hate creeps in and it's devastating–it can destroy you.

God so loved . . . God so loved the WORLD. When you consider what the world is and the type of people who make up this generation, this world, then you begin to understand how far beyond our loving the loving nature of God is. The love of God can only be understood in the measure of its love and what it loves. For God so loved the world that He gave. Now the measure of life is to give.

Husband, you may say, "I love my wife." And I say, if you love her, do you GIVE? Do you give yourself to your wife? If you do not, then you do not love your wife.

Wife, you do not love your husband unless you as a wife give yourself to your husband.

Young people, you say you love your parents but you cannot love your parents unless you are willing to give to them what a child should give to his parents.

For God so loved that He GAVE. And He gave . . . His only begotten Son.

ALL HAPPINESS IS DIRECTLY BASED ON THE MEASURE OF LOVE THAT WE GIVE

We human beings who try to live on an island are not happy. On the other hand, we human beings who give because we love, and give out of our love, achieve a measure of happiness because . . .

HAPPINESS IS GIVING . . .
GIVING IS LOVE AND
LOVE IS GOD.

God so loved that He gave . . . His only begotten Son. You always give your best. And you have never really given until you give something that costs you. Mary gave of the precious ointment which was worth so much money that Judas said, "Why was not this ointment sold . . . and given to the poor?" (John 12:5). And the Bible goes on to tell us, "This he said, not that he cared for the poor; but because he was a thief, and had the bag, and bare what was put therein" (John 12:6). That is, Judas was the treasurer for the disciples . . . he took care of their funds. He cared more for the funds than he did for people.

Parent, young person, you can solve your problems. You can close this spiritual gap between you when you look to Christ who is the Source of your supply. Through Christ you can learn to start giving first so that you may properly receive in return. Now is the time for you as a parent . . . for you as a young person . . . to ask God to come into your life and help you to give as Jesus taught you. I know in my heart that . .

PRAYER CHANGES PEOPLE AND PEOPLE CHANGE THINGS

Jesus said, "GIVE, FIRST." And there is no limitation set —it is a totality of giving. Give and keep on giving until you receive the miracle you need and keep on receiving it for your continuing need.

This reminds me of the woman who wrote me and asked, "Just how far do I have to go with this 'giving first'?" It seems that she had already filed for divorce—her marriage had been stormy for some time. Her husband would beat her so severely that at times the neighbors would call the police. Finally, in despair of his ever changing, she left him and filed for divorce.

Spiritually, mentally, and physically . . . she had come to the end of her rope. In her desperation she wrote me for prayer, and I wrote her back saying that I was praying for her and encouraging her to believe God for a miracle. In one letter I reminded her of the fishermen (Luke 5) who had toiled all night and taken nothing, and then the Lord came along and said, "Let down your net . . . just one more time."

In her letter back to me, she said:

> Dear Brother Roberts:
>
> When your letter came I was in the same frame of mind as those fishermen must have been. I wanted

to believe but I hardly dared to. Then there were your words, "Let down your net—one more time." I'm crying as I write this letter. I want you to pray with me that my husband will accept Christ and that we can be reunited.

WITHIN DAYS THE MIRACLE BEGAN. I received another letter:

Dear Brother Roberts:

Just a few days after I sent you that letter, the miracle began. My husband came by and wanted to talk with me. We talked but got nowhere, so I said:

"Take me home. Let's hang it up."

Instead he drove to our pastor's home, which was a miracle because in times past he had told the pastor to stay out of our business. The pastor and his wife talked to us for two hours (while friends prayed).

Then my husband asked:
"What can I do to save our marriage?" Our pastor told him that he should begin by committing his life to Christ. Later we all knelt and prayed and he accepted Christ as his Savior. And he became a changed man. *God did give us a whole net full of miracles . . . We cancelled our divorce.* Today our home is full of love. How I thank you for your ministry and prayers.

Jesus Christ didn't ask anything from anybody until He had given to them first

. . . until He gave himself

. . . His life

. . . His time
. . . His talent
. . . His eternal love
. . . EVERYTHING He had.

God himself called His Son "the Seed of David." Jesus was a seed-sower first. And by His example we can learn that . . .

The way to a child's heart . . . to a parent's heart . . . to the heart of a husband or wife . . . is to give first —to put a seed in—to become a SOW-ER.

YOUR SOURCE

Now when you give something it is important that you don't expect to receive back from the person you give to. Your child . . . your parent . . . your spouse . . . is not your Source. He or she is only an instrument. God is your Source! Whatever you give must become an act toward God.

For it is God who reconciles parents and children.

It is God who changes people—both you and your child.

It is God who renews the love in our hearts for one another.

But it all begins with giving . . . and giving FIRST. And you can't do this without God's love. Surrender your life to Christ. Take Him into your life and into your heart as your personal Savior. Make Him the head of your home. Follow Jesus, give as He gave, love as He loved, let Him help you to forgive as He forgives. Then start expecting . . .

miracle . . .
after miracle . . .
after miracle!!!

You will receive.

5

How You Can Pray And Know That God Hears You

HAVE YOU EVER WONDERED how to pray? What to say to God? What God is like? How you could communicate with Him? How you could be sure that your prayers were answered? Well, the answers to many of these questions about prayer are found in this chapter. It is about a prayer that has become very dear to each of us . . . a prayer that we say at least once a week and sometimes every day. It is the prayer that Jesus taught His disciples to pray . . . and it is known as . . .

THE LORD'S PRAYER

There was one thing about Jesus that stood out to His disciples and that was His prayer life. They noticed that when Jesus prayed something happened! Now it wasn't like that when they prayed—something might or might not happen. Doubtless some of them didn't even *like* to pray. There was something about prayer that Jesus was always turned on when He prayed. Deeply impressed by the way He prayed, the disciples eagerly came to Jesus and said:

Teach us to pray . . . (Luke 11:1).

And Jesus began by saying:

After this manner therefore pray ye . . . (Matthew 6:9).

AFTER THIS MANNER. Now Jesus was not indicating that this was to be the disciples' sole prayer . . . or that those were to be the only words they were ever to say in prayer. It was not to be a substitute for their prayers. But Jesus meant that they were to pray after the FASHION of this particular prayer which we today call "The Lord's Prayer."

> *Our Father which art in heaven, Hallowed be thy name. Thy kingdom come. Thy will be done in earth, as it is in heaven. Give us this day our daily bread. And forgive us our [trespasses], as we forgive [those who trespass against us]. And lead us not into temptation, but deliver us from evil: For thine is the kingdom, and the power, and the glory, for ever. Amen* (Matthew 6:9-13).

Our Father . . .

Jesus began the prayer with "Our Father . . ." Now the word "Father" as it pertains to God was not used in a personal way by the people of the Old Testament, although God was referred to as a father. It was first used in a personal way by our Lord Jesus Christ. The term "Father" signified the closeness they had together. It meant that He and God the Father were intimately and personally related. This was the new dimension that Christ brought out of the Old Testament into the New Testament and into the NOW. He tells us to call God "Father," suggesting the closeness of our relationship with Him.

Many years ago I read a story about President Abraham Lincoln and his son Tad. One day Tad was outside the White House playing in the yard while his father was busy inside with the affairs of State. Little Tad apparently got into a fist fight and came out the loser. He ran into the White

House with his lip cut, his nose bleeding, and his clothes torn. When he got to his father's outer office there sat several members of the President's Cabinet waiting to see him. The little boy, sobbing, said, "I want to see my father . . . I want to see my father!"

The Secretary of the Treasury—in sort of a spirit of jest—spoke up and said, "You wish to see the President of the United States?"

And the little boy said, "I want to see my FATHER!"

"Well," he said, "I will take you in personally to see the Chief Executive Officer of the United States."

But the little boy again said, "I want to see my FATHER."

Then the Secretary of State spoke up and said, "Look, I'll take care of the lad . . . Son, I'll take you into the presence of the greatest diplomat in the whole world—the head of our nation."

The little boy just kept on sobbing, "I want to see my FATHER."

Finally, the Secretary of War said, "Son, I'll take you in to see the Commander in Chief of the armed forces of the United States of America."

And the little boy said, "I just want to see my FATHER!"

Everything these men said about Lincoln was true but to the little boy that head of state, that great diplomat, the Commander in Chief of the armed forces was his father. And he knew if he could just get in there to his dad—with his cut lip, bleeding nose, and torn clothes—that his father would put his arms around him, pull him up close, and things would be all right again.

Jesus indicated that this is the relationship that we have with God in prayer. We are to think of Him as "Our FATHER . . ."

I remember how foolish I was as a teen-ager in my relationship toward my parents. I turned them off. I turned away from the church and away from God. I went away—I mean I put as many miles between my home and me as I possibly could. I stayed away until the night I collapsed at a basketball tournament. There I lay . . . bleeding from my lungs, hemorrhaging with tuberculosis, and I didn't even know I had the disease. My coach picked me up, laid me in the back seat of his automobile, and said, "Son, I'm driving you back to your parents in Ada, Oklahoma."

When we arrived he got out, went up to the house, and knocked on the door. I heard him say to the man who answered, "Are you Reverend E. M. Roberts?"

And my father said, "Yes, I am. Is there something wrong?"

The coach said, "Yes, sir. I have your son Oral in the car . . . you'd better come."

My father quickly ran to the car. The coach opened the back door and my father looked in and there I lay. I always called my father Papa and I said, "Papa . . . Papa."

He said, "What's the matter, son?"

I said, "Papa, I've gone the last mile of the way."

Then Papa reached in, scooped me up in his arms, and carried me into the house and laid me on the bed. There stood my mother. She had on an apron and she just buried her face in it and sobbed. Father leaned over me and I looked up at him and I said, "Papa . . . Papa."

Well, Papa went to work making arrangements for the doctors to come and for me to get the proper medicine. Then he wrote letters to his friends who knew how to pray and asked them to pray that his baby boy would be healed.

There was something about my father that was so deeply a part of my life. I've always been close to my mother but . . . oh . . . there was a relationship I had with my father that I cannot put into words. He stood for affection . . . foı confidence . . . for protection . . . for love. He was especially near his children when they were ill . . . when they were in trouble.

PAPA! Jesus was saying to you and to me, "When you pray, say, Our Father . . . Our Papa . . . Our Daddy."

One day some parents brought their little girl to the hospital. She was seriously ill but not critical—at least they didn't think she was. They stayed with her for awhile and then went home. The next morning they came back, bringing some fruit and toys. As they entered the hospital and were walking down the corridor to her room a nurse rushed out. She wasn't expecting them at that moment. She was so upset and she blurted out, "Oh, I have bad news. The most terrible thing has happened. Just ten minutes ago your daughter passed away."

I tell you, it was such a crushing blow that the parents didn't know what to do. And the nurse didn't know what to say. Finally, she gathered herself together enough to suggest, "Perhaps you'd like to go into our hospital chapel and say a few words . . . or just sit there."

As they went in, she called the chaplain. He came right away and went in. He saw them sitting there in their deep grief and he was lost for words so he went to the altar and knelt. The only words he could find to pray were, "Our Father, who art in heaven . . ." He just kept saying it over and over . . .

"Our Father, who art in heaven . . .
Our Father, who art in heaven . . .
Our Father, who art in heaven . . ."

Then he got up, went back to where the parents were sitting, and said, "I know quite a bit of how you feel. I know what these things do to people. I've been through a lot of it myself. But you know, I'd like to encourage you to do something. Just tell God what you feel . . . even if you feel bad at God, just say, 'God, I feel bad at You.' "

They looked at him in consternation but he said, "Don't worry about saying what you feel. God is big enough to take it. HE'S BIG ENOUGH TO TAKE IT."

I like that because I think we should tell God like it is. It's all right to tell God how you feel.

If you feel rough, say so.

If you don't feel right about Him, say it.

If you feel like God has let you down, say it.

Get it out because He's your Father . . . your Papa . . . your Daddy. He understands how you feel. Above all, He cares. God is concerned about you. God loves you. HE LOVES YOU!!!

Which Art . . .

God is. Jesus said when you pray, pray to someone who IS . . . who never changes. The weather changes . . . people change . . . circumstances change . . . but God never changes. God exists . . . HE IS.

Listen, say to yourself over and over again, "God IS . . . God is in the NOW!"

Say, "If He is not here in the NOW, He has never been."

Say, "He is willing to help *me*!"

Say, "If He is not willing to help me, He has not been willing to help anybody. But He IS . . . and He WILL!!"

GOD IS! God is . . . in your total life—physical, material, spiritual. You have a seven-day-a-week life . . . seven-day-a-week needs . . . and you have a seven-day-a-week God. God is with you every moment, every day, everywhere. GOD IS!

In Heaven . . .

Now Jesus was not trying to locate God. He was using this term to express the ability and power of God to take care of us and our needs. On another occasion Jesus said:

> *I am come that they might have life, and that they might have it more abundantly* (John 10:10).

When Jesus spoke those words the world was filled with impossibilities. All around Him, Jesus saw people hemmed in by circumstances, disease, discrimination, poverty, fear, and failure. And He knew that IN HEAVEN there were resources for man's needs—

water for his thirst . . .
food for his hunger . . .
strength for his weakness . . .
riches for his poverty . . .
a kiss for his sorrow . . .
gladness for his misery . . .
and love for his loneliness.

So Jesus reached up and took heaven and kissed the earth with it and opened it and gave to the children of men. He came with outstretched hands filled with God's blessing, with an open heaven behind Him. He came into people's lives at the point of their need, performing miracles and setting them free.

So Jesus tells you when you pray to remember that God your Father is IN HEAVEN. And IN HEAVEN there is no shortage of any good thing. God's riches are laid end-to-end across heaven waiting to be given to you.

Hallowed Be Thy Name . . .

Jesus had a deep feeling about the name of God He

never used it irreverently . . . nor in vain . . . nor as an obscenity. In fact, Jesus never used an obscenity. He reverenced the name of the Father with great honor and love. And He said to you and to me, "When you pray, be sure that you have reverence for the name of God."

When I was in Moscow, Russia, a number of years ago I had an experience that gave me a new understanding of "reverence." Every day I saw a long line of people—perhaps two miles long—line up to visit the tomb of Lenin in Red Square. This was the man who brought communism to Russia. He is entombed there exactly as he died. His right hand is upon his chest and it's not open into a hand but it is closed into a fist, indicative to me of the violence with which he associated himself during his lifetime.

Each day people walk by on either side of his coffin to see his body. Soldiers stand guard over the casket—about three feet apart—no one is allowed to stop. The lines just keep moving. I decided to go one day. I caught just a glimpse of the dead Lenin as I walked by.

The thing that stood out most to me was the reverence with which these many, many Communists gave to their long dead leader. I mean they *reverenced* him.

Not far away is the house in which Lenin died. In the room where he spent his last moments everything has been left untouched. It is exactly like it was when Lenin died. There is the book that he was reading. You will be surprised to know it is a book about our Lord Jesus Christ—the one Lenin said he could not believe in. The book is open and it is lying there. However, because it is written in English, and most of the Russian people do not speak English, they look at the book, smile and pass on. They don't know that it is a book about Christ. They reverence Lenin as the dead leader of communism and on the other hand they pass by his book that is about the Christian faith.

Lenin died with his fist clenched in hatred.

Jesus died with His hand open in love and healing to every human being.

How much more should we reverence His name!

Many years ago in Tulsa there was a famous photographer who worked for our *Tulsa Daily World* newspaper. He was known from coast to coast. He also was a rather obscene man, according to his own testimony. He cursed, almost without realizing that he was cursing. It was a part of him. He had a habit of taking God's name in vain.

His wife became a Christian and she was very close to God. The name of Jesus was precious to her. She stood about all she could, then one day when Lee began to curse God she looked at him with the firmness that only a wife can have toward her husband and she said, "Lee, don't you ever do that again in my presence!"

He whirled around and said, "What do you mean?"

And she said, "Don't you ever curse the name of my Lord in my presence again. He changed my life—He gave me back my life. Although I love you, Lee, and I am your wife, Jesus of Nazareth means more to me and has done more for me than anyone."

A strange quietness came over Lee.

Years later when I got to know him he told me this story and he said, "Oral, when she said that, something went into my heart—not merely my mind but my HEART. The Holy Spirit convicted me of my sins. And I said to her, 'Honey, will you pray for me?' She did and I accepted Christ."

Later Lee gave up his photography and his position, and became an evangelist. You see, the name of God and the name of Jesus Christ meant something to Lee's wife. She didn't like to hear God's name used irreverently. His name was hallowed to her. And because she took a strong stand for the name of God her husband came to know Christ.

Thy Kingdom Come . . .

Jesus was very concerned about the nations . . . the kingdoms . . . that existed on the earth. But He was even more concerned about another kingdom . . . a higher kingdom . . . God's kingdom. And He taught us to pray, ". . . thy kingdom come." A newspaper story I read in the '50s illustrates what Jesus meant when He said this:

A British team of mountain climbers were trying to scale the heights of Mt. Everest. While they were climbing, their leader—by the name of Mallory—slipped and plunged hundreds of feet below into the snow and disappeared.

This, of course, broke up that particular team and they went back to London to give their report. As they spoke to a packed audience there was a screen behind them showing pictures of Mt. Everest and the different levels where they had climbed and the exact spot where Mr. Mallory lost his life. They talked about their great leader, the hardships that they had undergone—the cold, the winds, the snow. Then the man who was doing the most talking straightened up, turned toward the picture of Mt. Everest on the screen, and began talking to it as if it were a living thing. He said:

> "Mighty Mt. Everest, we tried to conquer you once and you beat us. We tried to conquer you the second time and you beat us. But we are going to conquer you because YOU CANNOT GET ANY BIGGER BUT WE CAN!"

This is what Jesus is saying. We live in earthly kingdoms. These kingdoms are only going to be so powerful—they are limited. Jesus lived in the Roman Empire, a kingdom of men that had spread over the then-known world. It had conquered the nations and had control over all the people who lived in them. But Jesus said that these kingdoms of men are not going to fully conquer everybody . . . these earthly kingdoms are not going to get any bigger but God's kingdom IS.

Thy Will Be Done In Earth As It Is In Heaven . . .

Every time you pray this, you are praying a revolutionary, radical prayer. You are praying for a new kind of kingdom to come into being. You are praying that what is IN HEAVEN will come to be . . . down here IN THE EARTH. And that starts with you . . . (*in* earth, the substance from which our bodies are made) with your repentance and love. *The will of God starts in heaven but it must be lived out in this earthen vessel.* This affects you where you are and as you are.

One day a couple came to a pastor because they knew he was a man who preached a lot about Jesus and about love. They said, "We love each other but don't feel that it is necessary to be married—we just live together but we have a great love. Now you preach love, pastor, and love is in the Bible. So can you tell us what's wrong with our living together if we love each other as we do?"

The pastor said, "Well, first of all, you have missed the whole point. Our Lord said, 'Thy will be done in earth as it is in heaven.' It's the will of God that people marry. Fornication and adultery are inventions of men. Divorce was given because of the hardness of men's hearts (Matthew 19:8) but marriage is the creation of God. So you've missed the whole point. You've got to live according to the will of God. The will of God is that you marry and that you do not defile your earthen body—this earthen vessel of your body is the temple of the Holy Spirit and the Bible says:

> *If any man defile the temple of God, him shall God destroy; for the temple of God is holy, which temple ye are* (1 Corinthians 3:17).

So you are cancelling out this so-called 'loving' because you are defiling your bodies and you are not living in the will of God."

I used to be afraid of the will of God. I thought if I did God's will that it would tie me in knots . . . it would restrict my life . . . that I'd never be able to do anything worthwhile. But . . . oh . . . when I began to do God's will, I really began to LIVE. You see . . .

THE WILL OF GOD IS FULL OF LOVE.

It means love in marriage . . . love for little children . . . love that builds a stable home.

It means love that deals right with our brother and our sister in our family, and with other families and races.

It means loving ourselves and respecting ourselves too.

So the most important question we can ask ourselves is, "Am I doing God's will *in* earth as well as in heaven?"

I remember in 1947 when God spoke to my heart and said:

> "Now is the time to take My healing power to your generation."

People didn't understand. Not even my own beloved parents understood. They began to ask me many questions and I said, "You are asking the wrong questions. The important question is, 'Is it God's will?' Because if it is God's will I have to do it, and I have to find joy in doing it."

When we started to build Oral Roberts University there were all kinds of questions thrown at us: "Why? Are you sure? How?" But the only question I had to ask myself was. "Is it God's will?" And I knew it was.

Two outstanding men in this country—both ministers of the gospel—came to me. They were concerned about building a Christian college and they began to ask all kinds of questions . . . "What should we do? How do we go about it?"

I stopped them and said, "You are asking the wrong kind of question. The real question is, 'Is it God's will for you to start a college? Does God want you to do it?' "

They both had had properties given to them . . . properties already built and well suited for starting a college. I said, "When we began ORU we had nothing . . . just a pasture full of squirrels and rabbits. We had no money, no buildings, no faculty, no students. But I knew it was God's will for me to build a university. And I'd rather know it was God's will and start with NOTHING than NOT to know and start with a school already built."

Give Us This Day Our Daily Bread . . .

I'm glad Jesus didn't leave the bread out. The hip folks today call money "bread." They say, "Do you have any bread?" which means, "Do you have any money?" When Jesus said, "Give us this day our daily bread," He meant, "Give us this day our material needs." Jesus knew all about the physical necessities of life. He knew the worth of a widow's mite and what the loss of a coin meant to a housewife. He knew about clothes that needed mending and about not having a place to sleep at night.

Even after Jesus' resurrection He showed concern for His disciples' physical needs. The day He walked home with two of His friends He sat down at the table and broke bread with them. Several days later when the disciples had been out all night fishing, He knew that they would be hungry. So He prepared breakfast for them.

I'm glad Jesus didn't tell us to pray, "SELL us this day our daily bread," because we could never pay God. Instead Jesus said, "(GOD) *give* us this day . . ." You see, Jesus is saying that we can't get away from our Source. God is the Source of our total supply. We can never be very far away from our Source, who is God. The only true bread, the only true supply of our material needs comes through God.

Jesus is talking about bread . . . about GOD's BREAD. He's talking about a supply of our needs that really satisfies . . . about clothes that satisfy . . . about an automobile that works . . . about a house that becomes a home. He's talking about God meeting our needs.

God is concerned about your bread. He's concerned about money that you need . . . and the clothing you need . . . and the home you need. He's concerned about your physical health. He does not want you to die before your time. God wants you to have peace. He wants you to live out your days in health and happiness.

Forgive Us Our Trespasses As We Forgive Those Who Trespass Against Us . . .

After Jesus concluded the Lord's Prayer He added these words:

> *For if ye forgive men their trespasses, your heavenly Father will also forgive you: But if ye forgive not men their trespasses, neither will your Father forgive your trespasses* (Matthew 6:14,15).

Jesus indicated that the human race is guilty of trespasses . . . we are debtors. Each of us is a trespasser.

We DO things we ought not to do . . .
We SAY things we should not say . . .
We THINK things we should not think.

We are trespassers and our forgiveness must come from God. There is one Forgiver—and that is God. Men may or may not forgive us, but God WILL forgive.

> A man once said to John Wesley, "I'll never forgive." Wesley replied, "Then pray that you will never sin."

In other words, the only way you are ever going to be forgiven by God of your own trespasses is to forgive the one who trespasses against you.

When we were in England last year making a prime-time TV special, most of it was taped in the ruins of the Coventry Cathedral in Coventry. Now Coventry was one of the early sites to be bombed by Nazi Germany because it was an industrial city. They almost bombed it off the map and they didn't spare the churches. A bomb struck Coventry Cathedral—that tremendous edifice that was several hundred years old and beyond price—and destroyed it. Only a little of it was left standing.

When the war was over the people rebuilt the cathedral but they left the old, scarred, bombed-out part like it was. They took two pieces of scarred timber, put them together in the form of a cross and wrote on them . . . "Father, forgive" How could they forgive the Nazis? How could they forgive a people who killed six million Jews? How could they forgive a people who burned up their city? Destroyed their church?

In their hearts they reached a place where they said, "Father, forgive . . ." You see, they might have harbored some trespasses, also. They might have been hating back just as much as the Nazis hated them. So I believe it was a double prayer: "Father, forgive . . . (us and them)."

Many years ago we knew a family. The husband and wife fussed and quarrelled as they grew older. They made life miserable for each other. It seems that when couples get older that they sometimes do that. He was not a Christian but she was. However, she was acting the same way he did. One day the Holy Spirit convicted her heart and, in essence, said, "We sort of expect this behavior from a man who doesn't have Christ. But how can *you* do this? A Christian is to be a little Christ. (That's what the word Christian means . . . little Christ.) You are to be to your husband what Jesus would be through you."

So under the conviction of the Holy Spirit she went to her husband and said, "Honey, I know we've both said things that we should not have said but neither of us has a right—especially me. I have Christ in my life but I'm afraid I've not been a good disciple. I've not followed Him like I should. But I'm through with doing you the way I've been doing you and replying to you when you fuss. I ask your forgiveness."

Well, this made him sort of awkward and nervous and self-conscious. He didn't say much but she said again. "Now I forgive you and I will never again do this. I want you to forgive me . . . at least I'm asking you to."

The next seven or eight days were the sweetest of their entire marriage. Then suddenly he passed away. At the funeral as she stood, seeing his body lying in the casket, she was heard to say, "Darling husband, I'm so glad I asked you to forgive me. I'm so glad that we didn't fight and fuss anymore."

Later she said she didn't know whether or not he had accepted Christ during those last few days, but she believed that he had.

**Lead Us Not Into Temptation
But Deliver Us From Evil . . .**

In other words, Jesus said when we pray we should say, "God, don't forsake us when the going gets rough. Don't let us get into situations that are bigger than we are. Don't let us get into water over our heads."

I'm going to tell you a funny story but it makes a point. A fellow was asked where he was going and he said, "I'm going to get drunk and how I dread it!" You see, he wasn't enjoying drinking . . . he wasn't enjoying doing these terrible things to himself but they had a hold on him. He wanted God's help and that's what he was saying when he said, ". . . and how I dread it." It was a prayer. Now it may not sound like a prayer but a prayer can be just a sigh—or a groan. Or it may be a deluge of tears.

A man who came to me for prayer broke down and began to cry. As he tried to regain his composure he apologized, saying, "Mr. Roberts, I'm sorry. I know a grown man shouldn't cry but I can't help it." I encouraged him to let his tears flow. I told him they were a release for his spirit and an expression of his prayer to God.

Tears are not a sign of weakness, nor do they show a lack of manliness. Christ was a man's Man, and the Bible speaks of occasions when He wept. In the Garden of Gethsemane He prayed with "strong crying and tears" (Hebrews 5:7).

In whatever way we express the sincere desire of our heart to God He will understand and He will help us.

**For Thine Is the Kingdom,
and the Power,
and the Glory, Forever.
Amen.**

When Jesus said these words He was living in an outpost

of the Roman Empire. The Roman soldiers in their barbaric cruelty were everywhere putting their burdens on the people. They were acting like they were going to rule forever . . . that Rome would always be the master kingdom. But Jesus looked beyond Rome . . . beyond every other kingdom that would arise on the earth . . . and He said, ". . . THINE is the kingdom."

That is, Jesus was saying that there is something bigger and better and more stable than this or any other earthly kingdom . . . and that kingdom is ruled by the King of kings and the Lord of lords. He was saying to you and to me:

> "You are not alone. You are surrounded by the kingdom of God . . . an incomparable power that can set you free . . . a glory that can fill your breast. So why settle for the transient things of this world when you can have the permanent kingdom of God within you? You can have the limitlessness of the Spirit of God helping you to receive health again . . . you can have your soul saved . . . your material needs met . . . and this can start today."

6

How Your Trust In God Can Bring A Miracle Of Healing Into Your Body

THE MOST EXCITING POSSIBILITY in life is to know that YOU CAN BE HEALED. You can become a WHOLE person . . . complete in personality . . . in spirit . . . in mind . . . and in body. God can make a real restoration in your life. In this chapter I want to share with you HOW you can receive a miracle of healing for the affliction in your body.

I want to tell you about one of the most dramatic miracles of healing in Jesus' ministry. It is found in the eighth chapter of Matthew.

The scene is Capernaum. This chief city of Galilee was located at one of the crossroads of the ancient world leading from the East to the City of Rome. Sitting there on the shore of the Sea of Galilee, Capernaum was a great metropolis at that time, a center of trading. Here also was likelihood of revolt against Rome. So living there in charge of 100 Roman soldiers was the Centurion.

This was also the second home of Jesus. Early in His ministry Jesus had moved a few miles down the road from Nazareth to Capernaum. He made it His official headquarters the rest of His life. Here He performed some of His mightiest miracles and preached many of His greatest sermons. Here He walked the streets preaching deliverance by the power of

God and healing the sick by His word or by the touch of His hand. He stirred the city.

When Jesus first came and the Centurion saw that He had such magnetic power over the people . . . going among them, speaking the words of life, calling the people to repentance, and healing the sick . . . he was suspicious and hostile. He was afraid of any man who had such power as Jesus of Nazareth for he had been trained to spot such potential troublemakers. Day after day he watched Jesus and his feelings changed. It was not long until the Roman army captain realized that he had no grounds for his fears. He saw that . . .

Jesus was not against *any* man.

He was not against the Romans.

He was not against the Greeks.

He was not against the Jews.

JESUS WAS FOR PEOPLE!!!

He came not with a life-shortening suggestion but with a life-saving power. The Roman army captain realized that this was a different kind of man. He had never seen His equal before . . . either in Rome or in Palestine.

Then one day trouble struck the Centurion's family. One of his trusted and beloved aides was struck with paralysis—with shaking palsy—and he was desperately ill. The Centurion called for the Roman soldiers' physician—the physician of Caesar. He was not able to cure him. Although the Centurion was a captain of the great Roman army and was sent there by Caesar himself, there was nobody . . . anywhere . . . who could heal his servant. That's when he thought of Jesus of Nazareth.

This is when most people think of God . . .

when they are at the end of their rope . . .

when they have done all they can do . . .

when someone shakes his head and says,

"There's nothing more that can be done!"

Today you may have a pain in your body that you cannot explain. Or you may have trouble and heartbreak in your home. Or pressing financial obligations that are getting you down. I don't know what your problem is but I'm sure that you have one.

EVERYBODY HAS SOME KIND OF PROBLEM

You have a need in your life. If someone else can meet that need, all right. But if they *cannot* and the day will come when you have that kind of need . . .

when the physician will not be able to cure you . . .

the loan people will not be able to take care of your financial obligations . . .

no one will have the answer to the problems in your home—

then you will come face-to-face with the Man Jesus Christ. Just like the Roman army captain did two thousand years ago, you will meet this One who walks among us, whose name is Jesus Christ, this One who is the answer to our every need.

Now this Centurion faced a different kind of crisis. He wanted Jesus to heal his servant but he was a Roman and Jesus was a Jew. Now the Romans and the Jews did not fraternize with each other. In fact, the Romans were legally empowered to impose their obligations upon the Jews. For example, if a Roman were walking down the road and he met a Jew, he could legally force him to carry his load for one mile. Then he could even make him carry it a second mile. The Romans were the overlords and they were hated by the Jews.

Now this great gap between the Romans and the Jews got wider and wider in the Roman captain's mind. He sees that the only hope for his servant is in this Man Jesus Christ, a Jew. The captain knows if he turns to Jesus that he will be turning away from Caesar. Now Caesar was not only Emperor, but he was also worshipped as a divinity. And the Centurion had never before bowed to any man except Caesar.

The captain knew if he went to Jesus and asked Him to heal his servant that he would be taking a great risk. If he were reported to Caesar he might lose his command . . . or even his life. In any case he was sure to meet with ridicule from his fellow officers and soldiers.

What a crisis! And there's always one! There's always someone or something to muddy the waters, to confuse the issue, to make you feel that it will be a critical step if you turn your life over to Jesus Christ.

So the Centurion struggled with the problem. But as he thought about it he also realized that he had never seen Caesar work a miracle. He had seen him wage war victoriously and enslave the humans of the world. But he had never seen him lift up someone who was ill or in torment.

Then the Centurion made a great decision. He came to Jesus . . . and in broad daylight. There in the street of Capernaum he knelt in the dust and the first word that came from his lips was, "Lord." He had never called any man Lord before and most of us have not either. LORD.

I want you to see this picture of this proud Roman army captain kneeling in the dust before the Galilean.

It is force bowing to meekness,
it is armed might before the unarmed.
It is the proud eagle of Rome
bowing down before the Lamb of God.
It is the uniform of war
bowing before the seamless robe.

The Centurion said, "Lord," and he confessed himself a sinner.

IT IS THE GREATEST MOMENT IN ANY

INDIVIDUAL'S LIFE WHEN HE KNOWS WHO HIS LORD IS, WHEN HE REALIZES THAT HE IS A SINNER . . .

when he comes to God for something physical or material and he realizes that there is another step to take first . . . and that is to transfer his allegiance to Jesus Christ.

Friend, I ask you . . . is Jesus Christ your Lord? In other words, who are you serving? To whom are you looking for salvation . . . or healing?

Have you taken Christ as your Savior . . . have you called Him LORD? Make that decision . . . make it early . . . make it in the NOW and live in the now of God's healing love for you.

Then the Centurion said, "My servant lieth at home grievously tormented." Now there's a lot in that statement. Oh, the grief and torment that we go through. I learned early in life that torment and grief are no respecter of persons. They strike young people just like they strike the older people. They strike the rich as well as the poor. They strike the powerful as well as the weak. And the hurt that young people feel is as much as an 80-year-old feels. The grief and torment that you feel when you are told that you are REALLY sick is the same, regardless of your station in life. I mean, when you are sick and you are told that you are not going to get well again it doesn't matter what your name is . . . or where your address is . . . or whether you are black or white, you hurt just the same. The grief of a problem that kicks you in the face, no matter which way you turn, hurts just the same, no matter who you are. We all feel these problems the same.

The Centurion said, ". . . he's grievously tormented." Now the statement of Jesus in reply to this man's statement is perhaps the greatest that you and I could ever hear in the NOW. It breaks me up. Jesus said:

I WILL COME AND HEAL HIM

NOW CHRIST WAS EITHER ON HIS WAY TO HEAL . . . OR HE WAS THERE HEALING . . . OR HE HAD JUST LEFT, AND THE PERSON WAS UP PRAISING GOD.

Jesus came to take off of you what the devil put on you . . .
to take out of you what the devil put in you . . .
to put back on you what the devil took off of you . . .
and to put back in you what the devil took out.

Jesus said, "I will come and heal him," and He's still saying it today. If you will listen you can hear His voice across the centuries saying, "I will come and heal him."

You see, Jesus talked about healing the *man*, the person. In our day we have great surgical skill and indeed this is a great gift of God. I believe God heals through surgery, through medicine, and other techniques. But listen, at the very best, most of this work seems to be done with the sickness itself. But this Man Jesus comes to heal the person who is sick. He says, "I will come and heal him."

Now when we are ill we sometimes think that we are ill in our bodies . . . or in our minds . . . or in our souls. But Jesus teaches us that when one part of us is sick that the whole man is sick. If there is something wrong in the body, it affects the mind . . . it affects the soul. Or if there is something wrong in the soul of man, it affects his mind and his body as well.

Sometime ago a friend of mine said, "Oral, I've been wanting to tell you something. Two years ago I had a stinging pain in my body and I went to my doctor. He and other doctors worked over me for some time and finally became so concerned that they sent me to Mayo Clinic. I was there for several weeks. I got worse. I became depressed and afraid. Then one day my doctor came in and said to me, 'Mr. Black, do you believe in prayer?'

"Well, yes, I pray when I'm in trouble."

"Then the doctor looked at me and said, 'Mr. Black, you're in trouble now.' And he left the room.

"I turned over and began to pray. I knew there was something wrong . . . very wrong. But as I prayed, a calm came over me and I went to sleep. When I awakened the stinging pain had gone out of my body. I called the doctor and he released me and I came back to Tulsa. Oral, that was two years ago and I haven't suffered that pain since. I'M A NEW MAN."

This man found that he was not just a body; he had a soul. He was a *person* and God had dealt with him that way.

JESUS IS A WHOLE-MAN HEALER

Until you are healed by Jesus you can never be completely healed. You may have a successful surgery . . . you may come out of some problem, but you are never healed in the *whole* man until Jesus heals you.

The Centurion said:

> *Lord, I am not worthy that thou shouldest come under my roof: but speak the word only, and my servant shall be healed. For I am a man under authority, having soldiers under me: and I say to this man, Go, and he goeth; and to another, Come, and he cometh; and to my servant, Do this, and he doeth it* (Matthew 8:8,9).

In other words, the Centurion said, "Lord, I'm not worthy that You should enter into my house. Besides, it is not necessary for You to come to my house in order for You to heal my servant. I see Your authority here but I am also a man under authority. I am sent here by Caesar and I've been given power and authority by Caesar. When I raise my hand

and speak, it is the word and authority of Caesar. But, Lord, You have power and authority above all power and authority. You don't have to come to my house. JUST SPEAK THE WORD ONLY AND MY SERVANT SHALL BE HEALED."

You know, when you drive your car down the street, and you come to an intersection, and a traffic officer is standing there, he is the most powerful man in the world as far as you are concerned. By a mere lifting of his hand and throwing it out toward you, he can make you put on the brakes and stop that automobile. Do you know why you stop? Because although he's a single solitary human being, and he is unable physically to force you to stop if you want to run your car over him, you stop because back of him are the citizens of your community . . . and back of them are the people of your state . . . and back of them are the 210 million people of the United States . . . and back of them are the army, the navy, and the air force. So when the officer puts up his hand and says, "Stop," you stop!!

Now, friend, that's authority! That's power!! Jesus is seen in an even greater light than that and the Centurion says, "You have power ABOVE ALL POWER. Back of my power is the authority of Caesar but even that cannot make the sickness of my servant go. But, Lord, You have authority and power over ALL sickness. You can say the word . . . You can speak the word . . . You can tell the sickness to go and it will go."

Now that's respect for authority. And nobody—nobody—can live for Christ unless he respects the authority of the living Christ . . . until the living Christ becomes his Lord and beside Him there is no other . . . so that when Christ speaks, he obeys. If He tells us to kneel, we kneel. If He says to run, we run. If He tells us to go, we go.

JESUS CHRIST HAS AUTHORITY ABOVE ALL AUTHORITY

When Jesus speaks to a disease . . . it leaves!
When He speaks to a financial obligation . . . it is solved!
When He speaks to a marriage that is falling apart . . . it is healed!

And the authority of this Man Jesus is as much in the present as it was back then. That same compelling voice is being spoken to people today who recognize His authority.

Then Jesus said, in essence, "I've traveled throughout the length and breadth of Israel . . . I've been in the synagogues and in the temple itself, but I'VE NOT FOUND SO GREAT FAITH, NO NOT IN ISRAEL!! And I say unto you, that many shall come from the East and from the West and the Gentile worlds. They will sit down in the kingdom with Abraham, Isaac, and Jacob. But you Hebrew people—you who are the children of the kingdom, you who have the light—will be cast into outer darkness where there will be weeping and wailing and gnashing of teeth."

Why did Jesus say this? Because most of the people did not recognize His authority. He could speak the word and it was mere words to them. He could talk among them as the Son of God and it was as though He were an ordinary mortal. They didn't recognize His authority. He could walk among them as the Son of God and it was as though they didn't recognize that . . .

He was the Fount of all life . . .
the Source of all power . . .
the Giver of all gifts . . .
the Creator of every living thing . . .
the very Son of the living God.

But they didn't recognize Him. So they turned away and refused to accept His authority. As a result Jesus said that the light they had would be turned into darkness.

Jesus said, "I have not found so great faith . . ." Jesus was telling you and me today that there is only one way to start having great faith and that is to start recognizing that God's authority is over *all* of life and that His Power is above *all* power. To have great faith we've got to bring ourselves under His authority . . . we've got to make Him LORD of our life . . . to choose His will rather than our own. Jesus says that such believing is GREAT FAITH. This faith reaches out to God and brings miracles into our existence to meet our most desperate needs.

Then Jesus turned to the Roman army captain and said:

> *Go thy way; and as thou hast believed, so be it done unto thee* (Matthew 8:13).

Now that's what the captain was waiting for. He was not waiting for the Lord Jesus to come to his house . . . he was waiting for Him to SPEAK a few words . . . GO THY WAY. AS THOU HAST BELIEVED, SO BE IT DONE UNTO THEE. These words were his point of contact.

WHAT IS A POINT OF CONTACT?

A point of contact is something you do and when you do it you release your faith. Now faith is inside you. "God hath dealt to every man the measure of faith" (Romans 12:3). Faith is something you have . . . but until you release it, it is as though you have none.

A man said to me, "Brother Roberts, I have all the faith in the world."

I said to him, "That's your problem, you STILL have it!"

And I was sincere. The faith you have has to be released.

It has to come out of you. It has to become an act, a single act of believing. It was no accident that Jesus said to the captain, "GO thy way and as thou hast BELIEVED, it shall be done unto thee." *Believed* is a word of action. It was as if Jesus had said, "As you ARE BELIEVING, it shall be done." Faith has to act. It has to come out of your heart and a point of contact helps you to release your faith.

Now the captain's point of contact was the WORD of Jesus. He said in so many words, SPEAK THE WORD, SAY IT, LORD. THAT'S WHEN I'LL LET MY FAITH GO TO GOD.

I often say when I write a letter, "This letter is anointed, use it as a point of contact to release your faith to God for your healing." I especially remember one woman who did this.

She had been prayed for many times and had received the laying on of hands but still she was not healed. Then one day she sat down and wrote a letter to me. It was just a few lines telling me of her disappointment. She wanted me to read her letter, to say a prayer for her, and to write her back telling her that I had done so.

She said, "I've come to the place I no longer am looking to you or to any other person, just the Lord."

Well, of course, I read her letter, I prayed, and I wrote her back. In my letter to her I said:

> "As I pray I feel God's power going through me, therefore, this letter has His Spirit upon it. Lay it on your body as a point of contact and let your faith go to God. BE HEALED IN JESUS' NAME."

In a short time here came back a three-page letter from her to me full of praises to God. She told how she had read my letter and as she held the letter in her hand she said to the

Lord, "Your Spirit is in Oral Roberts; I feel it in this letter. As I place it on my body I am expecting You to give me a miracle. I am expecting a miracle of healing."

Then she said, "Something that felt like a warm liquid started flowing through my entire being. I felt strength, well-being, joy. I knew from that moment on that God was healing me . . . and He has."

I thought, Lord, what this woman did, others can do if they will just look to YOU, the Source of all healing power. I believe this with all my heart.

THE POINT OF CONTACT IS SOMETHING YOU DO

Oh, I want to stress that. It's something YOU do. It is simply like going over to the light switch. The light switch is connected to the power house but you do not need to turn the power house on. You are going to turn the switch on . . . and the switch is the point of contact. You flip on the light switch and things begin to happen. The current is released from the power house and it begins to flow down the line and the lights come on.

Your point of contact may be laying your hand on my letter . . . or joining hands with someone at the close of the telecast when I pray. When you do this, it focuses your faith on your Source, God.

IT SETS THE TIME FOR YOUR HEALING

There was a couple in El Paso, Texas. The wife had been in and out of bed for eight years and finally she was unable to even do her housework. So the husband had to work all day and then come home and do the housework. There they were. He said they were not church people. They were away from God, they had no Source for their lives. There they were

—just sort of cut off with their problems. They hadn't really even thought about God entering into their lives.

They had had the best that medicine had to offer but they still wound up with the same problem. Then they began watching our telecast and they began to think about God the healer. One day I preached about the point of contact and the husband caught on to the idea . . . SET THE TIME . . . SET THE TIME. He decided that at the close of the telecast when I prayed, that would be their time. So they listened to me preach and when the time came to pray, I asked each one to touch someone there in the room with them as a point of contact. This was strange to them. They had never touched each other in connection with prayer. But the more you turn yourself to God, the more you will turn to one another. Have you ever thought about that? There they sat touching one another, trying to pray, and neither one of them was a Christian. But he said, "During the prayer when you prayed you said, 'Now is the time! Release your faith and BE HEALED!' I felt a warmth start flowing through me. My wife looked at me and said, 'Honey, something happened to me,' and I said to her, 'It's happening to me too.'

"Brother Roberts, today my wife is so much better. She is now able to do her own housework. She's not yet completely well but we believe she will be. We're both serving the Lord now and we're learning how to use our faith every day. THIS IS REAL. THIS IS REAL!!"

Now it's so very important that you set the time to release your faith. If I said to you, "I will meet you," and you said, "OK, Oral Roberts, when?"

And I said, "Anytime."

And you said, "Where?"

And I said, "Anywhere," it is doubtful if we would ever meet. On the other hand, if I said I'd meet you here in my office at ORU at such and such a time on a certain day, and you agreed to come, then we would meet.

When you come to Christ to be healed, your faith must come out of you.

People are always saying to me, "Must I have faith?"

In nine out of ten cases I would say, "Yes." There is that exception when the sovereignty of God overrules and He will heal you. In those cases, we cannot explain how it happens.

I urge people everywhere to get it out of their minds that God works magic. Get it out of your mind that somebody has personal healing power. The best of us are only instruments. All healing is in the Lord. Therefore, we must turn ourselves toward the Lord. He must become our Lord, our way of life . . . our LIFE.

A miracle is not something for nothing. It doesn't happen by our doing nothing. A miracle comes through faith and particularly through Seed-Faith (Matthew 17:20). A miracle comes through seeding for a miracle . . . when you put in the seed of your life . . . of your faith (Key No. 2 of Seed-Faith). A miracle comes when you act upon your faith.

The Bible says this:

> *His servant was healed in the selfsame hour* (Matthew 8:13).

I want you to notice that his servant was HEALED. I know there are many sincere people who believe that when they are prayed for they are healed—whether they are or not. They still have the same affliction but they say, "I'm healed . . . the symptoms have just not left."

Possibly this is so. However, that's not the kind of healing that Jesus brought to the Centurion's servant. He was healed! Friend, when Jesus heals you, you are healed!! You can put it down for a fact. Even the symptoms will leave.

WHEN YOU GET A GENUINE HEALING FROM THE LORD YOU ARE HEALED!!

PRAYER

Now I want to pray for you. And I'm going to ask you to accept the words of Christ in Matthew 18:19 where He said, "If two of you shall agree on earth as touching any thing that they shall ask, it shall be done for them of my Father which is in heaven." TOUCH AND AGREE. I'm going to ask you to touch someone or to think of someone who needs help—who needs a miracle. If you are there alone put your hand on this book as a point of contact. Or maybe you'll just want to wrap your arms around yourself and think about somebody who needs a touch from God. Let's look to God as we pray:

Father, we come to you not in our own strength or in our own power, but in the matchless name of Your Son Jesus Christ of Nazareth.

And now, Lord, for this person who has a deep problem in his home, I come against this problem, this friction, this discord, in the name of Jesus. I adjure it to leave by the living God. Lord, give Your servant victory over this problem. Give deliverance. Give a miracle.

And now, Jesus, I ask You to rebuke the devil and cast out this financial problem. Bring in the finances that our partner needs to meet this overwhelming need. Devil, I command you to take your hands off God's property.

Now, Jesus, here is our sister and she has this affliction. You said, "I will come and heal . . ." So I'm asking You now to heal her. Oh, my sister, be healed! Experience the healing Christ as He touches you from your head to your feet. Be healed in your whole being.

My brother, as you carry this affliction in your body

remember that our Lord took it in His own body. I'm asking Jesus now to heal you. My brother, be healed. Be healed from the crown of your head to the soles of your feet. Through Christ, I believe and I expect many miracles.

My child, I pray for this sickness or this problem that makes you troubled and hurt deep inside. I pray that Jesus of Nazareth—the same Man who took the little ones up in His arms and blessed them—will touch you and bless you today. Be healed.

Now, Father, let the healing of the Lord continue to flow through this person's body.

We touch and agree in the name of Jesus of Nazareth. And I pray that a miracle will happen to you. Amen and amen.

7

How You Can Live Without Fear In Today's World

THERE IS A FEAR in this country right now . . . a panic . . . an almost frantic feeling about the high cost of living. This fear is beginning to get into the subconsciousness of people, way down in their souls. People are worried, fretting about high uncontrollable prices. After a while they develop a complex of negativism until God is almost blotted from their minds.

I feel this fear in the letters I receive. People write to me that they don't know what's going to happen to them next. Some of these dear people have good incomes, some are broke and without a job. Some are working at hard jobs day after day just to make ends meet. Some are filled with fear even though they are very successful. Others are afraid they're not going to make it at all.

Many people fear for their families and for their children.

People are afraid of war.

Some are afraid of what's happening in our government and in our cities.

People are afraid of living and dying.

Some are afraid for their health.

It seems that everybody is afraid of *something*.

BUT WHAT ABOUT YOUR LIFE? Have you felt the hot

searing pain of fear in the pit of your stomach? Do you ever become afraid until you don't know where to turn, you don't know what to do, you don't know what to say?

Well, there's an answer for the fear in our land and for the fear and anxiety in your own life. Let me share that answer with you from my own experience and from the Bible—God's Holy Word.

GOD IS NOT THE AUTHOR OF FEAR

First, let me say that God does not want us to be afraid—to let fear dominate our lives. Fear does not come from God.

In Luke 1:74,75, our Lord says that He will deliver us out of the hand of our enemies that we might serve Him without fear all the days of our life. In 2 Timothy 1:7 we see another powerful Scripture, GOD HATH NOT GIVEN US THE SPIRIT OF FEAR: BUT OF POWER, AND OF LOVE, AND OF A SOUND MIND. Fear comes from the devil—it paralyzes the spirit and mind of God's children and keeps them from reaching out to God as the Source of their lives.

SIN IN OUR LIFE BRINGS ANXIETY AND GREAT FEAR.

Let's go back to the Bible. Let's go back to the first man, Adam, who became afraid and went and hid himself from God.

"Adam, why did you become afraid?"

"Because I sinned. I was ashamed and afraid, and I hid myself."

He could not face God with hidden sin in his life. His sin burdened him with great anxiety and fear.

I read about a man who had a little illegitimate child—a little girl—and he tried to keep it a secret. He kept this from most of his family for many years. But when the child was

16 years old she fell in love with his own grandson and one of the members of the family got drunk and told all about it. It tore that family apart. Fear struck them and for weeks they lived in fear. Why? Because something back there had not been faced—something had not been brought to God, their Source. Now that's what the Bible says can happen. *If you are fearful it may be because there's something in your life that you need to open up and tell to God.* Face it squarely. Repent (change your mind) about it. Doing this is one of the best ways to get rid of guilt.

GIVE YOUR PAST WITH ITS MISTAKES AND FAILURES TO GOD

The Bible says:

> *As far as the east is from the west, so far hath he removed our transgressions from us* (Psalm 103:12).
> *Thou wilt cast all their sins into the depths of the sea* (Micah 7:19).

The first time I went around the world I started in the West. I never reached the East because the earth is round. In these Scriptures God talks about the endless circle of His love. When you confess your sin and accept Jesus Christ as your personal Savior, your sins are forgiven. God casts them into the depths of the sea, never to be remembered against you again.

If you are not careful you can become so upset about your past that it will destroy you. *Hidden guilt will crush you; it will rob you of your faith.* It will prevent you from making your own demonstration of Seed-Faith living through the 3 MIRACLE KEYS. Bring your guilt, your past sins, out into the light of God's love. Repent of your past and give it to

God—He will erase it. Then, and only then, can you face the future unafraid.

FEAR COMES WHEN WE FORGET WHO OUR SOURCE IS

I dealt with a man not long ago who wanted to be employed in our ministry. He had much to offer and believed very much in what we were doing, but when we came down to it he said, "I don't think I can handle it."

I wanted to know *why* because I felt he was eminently able and qualified.

He said, "It would require too much mental revamping to learn to depend upon God as my Source. Where I am I know how much I earn. No matter what happens I'm taken care of. I don't fear the future. *I've got security.* At my age I've got to think about security for my family."

THE MOST DANGEROUS TIME IN OUR LIVES IS WHEN WE DO NOT HAVE TO HAVE FAITH . . . WHEN EVERYTHING IS TAKEN CARE OF

I thanked him nicely for even considering us and wished him Godspeed. I wish I could have talked with him more because I think he's in one of the most dangerous periods of his life. I think most people are in a dangerous period of their life when they feel that they have to stay at a place where there's no risk to be taken . . . where they don't have to cast out in faith upon God . . . where they feel that everything is going to be provided for them through good and bad times . . . where they don't have to have faith. We are in a dangerous period when that feeling is in our hearts.

Your greatest source of supply and sense of security is in the things you lack . . . not in the things you have. For the things you have, if you are not careful, can become a god to you and you will lean on them. You might say:

"I've got a good job, everything is OK."

Or:

"I've got a good marriage, nothing will ever happen to it."

"I have wonderful children, they will never go wrong."

"I'm doing fine. I'm OK. No matter what happens I'm OK."

But when you do this you are leaning upon something of this world and God is left out. When we lean on material things—on our job, the money we have in the bank, etc.—we lose something. We lose the sense of trust in God.

GOD HAS SO DESIGNED US THAT WE MUST DEPEND UPON HIM—HE IS THE SOURCE OF OUR LIFE

I have this problem all the time. I never have enough money. We raised the salary of our faculty here at Oral Roberts University and in three months' time the cost of living had gone up so much that the raise seemed to be lost. These faculty members are human beings—wonderful Christian men and women, but I could see fear sweeping in. It was like they were thinking, *what am I to do? I am locked in now to this salary for another year. I'm afraid things will keep going up until my family will be in need.* Then they think of me. Here I am, the president of a university that was built out of nothing. And we still start buildings with no money. We have several buildings under construction now. We started them with very little money and we don't have money to complete them.

You talk about getting scared and getting frantic. I have no institution back of me, no group to turn to, and it's hard, but it's wonderful. Oh, I hurt and I get scared and I get nervous. Don't misunderstand me. It's wonderful because it puts Oral Roberts down on his knees and he has to say, "God, if You don't help me, I cannot finish the building. God, if You don't help me I cannot pay the faculty. God, if You don't help me I will completely fail."

We help a lot of our students and they are worried sometimes when they don't have the money to pay all their tuition, board and room, and sometimes we have to help them. But where does our help come from? I mean, where—where do we turn? I tell you where we turn–down on our two knees. Others on this campus get on their knees too, and partners of ours around the world get on their knees and we learn to trust in God.

As a matter of fact, if God would permit someone to walk in and just offer us all the money in the world, it would be the worst thing He could do to us because it would take away our sense of trust in God.

I tell you, and I tell you as an individual, you've got to quit worrying about the high cost of living. You've got to quit worrying whether someone is treating you right or not. You've got to doubt your doubts and believe your beliefs! You've got to start thinking about God and your relationship with Him . . . of whether you have made Him the Source of your supply or whether you have made some man your source or some company your source or yourself your source. The only good source . . . the only good security . . . is God.

Let me tell you, *with God your needs are His.* You are God's property and God watches out after his property. The most important thing you can know is that GOD CARES ABOUT YOU!

LEARN TO TRUST YOUR SOURCE

A crack airline pilot almost failed his first solo flight because he didn't trust his plane. He got off the ground, up in the air, but then the instructor saw the plane begin to wobble and dip. He ran frantically back and forth on the field, signaling the pilot to land. Finally he somehow made a landing.

"What in the world were you doing up there?" the instructor asked.

"I tell you, sir, I just couldn't rest my full weight on the seat. When I got up there and saw how big the sky was and how little my plane was, I just couldn't see how it could fly. To tell the truth, I was getting up and down, bumping my head against the ceiling—I just couldn't sit still and trust it."

The instructor said, "That airplane is MADE to fly. You don't have to fly it—just adjust the instruments, put your full weight down on the seat and it will fly itself!"

How many times have we done the same thing with God? We say God is our Source, but by our actions we say that we aren't quite sure we can trust Him.

God is saying to us, "I am your Source. You can TRUST ME. Lean back on Me. *Put your full weight on Me.*"

Rest your full weight on God, "casting all your care upon him; for he careth for you" (1 Peter 5:7). I know it's not easy. I'm not going to say that it is but I know that it can be done. Every one of us has done it at some time, haven't we? But we need to learn to do it more and more often and for longer periods of time. As we do, our fear will decrease and our faith will increase. Now say it with me:

**GOD IS THE SOURCE OF MY TOTAL SUPPLY . . .
I REST MY FULL WEIGHT ON HIM**

I tell you, I'm striking at the root of the problem today. We think important things are unimportant. DO YOU KNOW THE MOST IMPORTANT THING IN YOUR LIFE IS THAT GOD CARES FOR YOU . . . GOD CARES FOR YOU!

If you need a job, I think God is concerned.

If you can't buy enough groceries to feed your family, I think God is concerned.

If there's trouble in your home . . . in your relationships

with your husband . . . your wife . . . your children, I think God is concerned.

I also think God is concerned about the world, about humanity, about pollution, about civil rights—but more important, He cares about you as a person and where you are right now in this moment of your existence.

EVERYTHING about you is important to God. GOD REALLY CARES ABOUT YOU. This God who is your Source of supply really cares about you. He really cares!! God cares about you and me.

GOD'S CONCERN IS TOTAL AND GOD'S PROVISION IS TOTAL

In Habakkuk 3:17,18,19, God is saying that if all the crops fail and all the jobs fail and all the things fail that have to do with your material life, you can still rejoice in God. You can look to God who is your strength and your Source. You can go through all of this without fear of things to come, without losing your faith, without being denied the things that you have to have.

The devil will send all types of hindrances in our lives . . . either through our associates, relatives, our loved ones, or strangers. There will always be someone to try to cut us down. To rob us of our faith. To turn our eyes away from God and to make us feel there is no hope. But ringing through the centuries, until we can hear His voice in our consciousness today, are these words of Jesus: "Fear not, believe only." FEAR NOT, BELIEVE ONLY.

Don't mix your faith with doubt.
Don't listen with your doubt.
Don't listen with your fears.
Listen to God with your faith.

8

How To Cope With The Death Of A Loved One

THE BIBLE SAYS, "It is appointed unto men once to die, but after this the judgment . . ." (Hebrews 9:27). Yet death seems always to come unexpectedly. We never seem to be ready for it—not even Christians. We sometimes are touched so deeply that we almost lose our moorings, our contact with reality. This is so true today in the kind of world that we live in—wars and rumors of war, famine, riots and violence, and everything that is swirling around us. We need to be reminded that Jesus knows all about these things—and He cares. He himself was touched by death and He is our answer.

I remember the first time I felt the infinite sadness that death brings. It was in the forties when President Franklin D. Roosevelt died. A stab of pain shot across America. In the little town where I lived I saw the sorrow of the people. Then in November 1963 young President John F. Kennedy was killed while in office—his death made worse by an assassin's bullet. His brilliant young life was cut down by death and millions of people wept openly. And I thought of death again . . . of its meaning on the most personal level.

Thornton Wilder, the great playwright, has these words in one of his plays: "Everybody knows in their bones . . .

there's something way down deep that's eternal about every human being."

In spite of the brokenness of death we know that because of the resurrection of Christ there is the possibility of the continuity of life. In spite of the separation of our soul from the body at death we have the confidence that we shall live again through Jesus Christ, our Lord.

JESUS TALKS ABOUT DEATH AS WELL AS LIFE BUT JESUS IS LIKE THAT—HE DEALS IN REALITIES

It's interesting to me that the Gospel of John concerns mostly the last five months of the life of Jesus. It talks a great deal about Christ's passion. About death. Some people object to the Gospel of John because it speaks so much about death. But Jesus is like that. He deals in realities. He's where we are, where our need is. And He talks to us about our needs.

Remember, on the cross our Savior said, "Father, into thy hands I commend my spirit" (Luke 23:46). And He died. That is, His body died. Just before He died, a young thief on one of the other crosses cried out to Jesus for mercy and Jesus said, "To day shalt thou be with me in paradise" (Luke 23:43).

The Bible teaches that death to a Christian is instant transference. Instant. The moment death takes the body, at that instant we're absent from the physical body and at home with the Lord (2 Corinthians 5:8). And the Bible says, "We shall be like Him" (1 John 3:2).

What happens immediately thereafter? The Bible says, "Blessed are the dead which die in the Lord henceforth: Yea, saith the Spirit, that they may rest from their labours; and their works do follow them" (Revelation 14:13). The key phrase is *dying in the Lord.* Not only do we live in Christ but we also die in Christ. And immediately after death, this blessed transference takes place. In a sense, the greatest day in your life is not your birthday but your death day. Someday we'll understand that statement more fully.

Just before my father's death I went over to his house and sat on the side of the bed and took him in my arms. He was 86. By then he didn't weigh very much. I held him in my arms. My father and my mother led me to Christ and I was very close to my father. I was used to going over to their house and I would sit there with the Bible and talk and pray with him and ask his advice about different things in the Bible. It meant so much to me. But then I held him in my arms. And I said to my father (I always called him Papa), "How is it now, Papa?"

And Papa said, "Son, Jesus Christ is closer to me now than He has ever been. And when my body dies and all of you gather together I hope you'll say something to the people, son. I want you to tell them the good news of the gospel—that I lived it. And then invite people to come to Christ."

And at my father's funeral there were scarcely any tears. There was a feeling of joy. I stood up and talked about my father and his life as he lived it for Christ. And God helped me not to break down. Now that meant something. Of course, we all felt deep grief but the joy of the Lord sustained us in that difficult hour.

WHAT DO YOU DO TO OVERCOME GRIEF?

Well, grief is a fact. First of all, you have to accept it. You have to accept grief as a fact because there's no easy way to give up a little child or a wife or a husband or a father or a mother. There's no easy way. It hurts. You have to accept it. We can't act like it's strange; it's a fact. But we don't have to live with that grief. Because at that moment we can turn outward. We can become involved in the needs of other people. You can find the reality of what Jesus said, "Give, and it shall be given unto you" (Luke 6:38).

Jesus could talk to us about death . . . He could show us how to cope with death because He personally had to face it. JESUS DIED! Now He didn't *have* to die. He could have called twelve legions of angels down to deliver Him from death. He could have been set free by Pilate, the Roman governor, who during His trial offered the release of a prisoner. If Jesus had only said the right words the mob would have chosen Him. But He chose to stand by His convictions and they chose a murderer, Barabbas, instead.

JESUS WRESTLED WITH THE POSSIBILITY OF HIS OWN DEATH

It was in the Garden of Gethsemane, the dark night before Jesus' crucifixion, that He, in His humanity, wrestled with the possibility of His own death. You know, He was God in the flesh, God incarnate. He was so much God it was as if He were not man. Yet He was so much man, it was as though He were not God. There Jesus knelt, feeling what we experience about death, and He prayed about death. He said, "O my Father, if it be possible, let this cup [of death] pass from me . . ." (Matthew 26:39). As He prayed and struggled with himself His sweat became like great drops of blood that fell down to the ground (Luke 22:44). Finally Jesus said, "Nevertheless not as I will, but as thou wilt" (Matthew 26:39). He who did not deserve to die went to the cross to die for those who did. He took death upon His being . . . into His very existence . . . and faced it for you and me.

Sometime ago I heard about an American missionary woman in Korea. She had become a friend of a large family there. The oldest girl was going to have a baby. As the girl neared the time of the birth of her child, she decided to walk the several miles to the missionary home where she would receive aid. It was a bitterly cold and freezing day. She came to a long bridge and as she was crossing it the birth pains hit her. She knew her time had come so she crawled down under the bridge and there she gave birth to a little baby son. She had no blankets or garments to wrap the baby in so she stripped off her own clothes and wrapped her infant son in them.

The following day the missionary had to make a trip and when she was coming back over this road, driving her jeep, she ran out of gas. She got out to look around to see what she could do when she heard a faint cry. It seemed to be coming from under the bridge. Quickly she searched and there she found the baby boy wrapped up, hungry and crying, but still alive. Beside him was the naked body of his mother, frozen to death.

The missionary adopted the little boy as her own son. As he grew up she told him of the death of his mother and how she had died to give him life. When he was twelve years old, he said to the missionary, "I want you to take me to the bridge. I want to see where my mother died to give me life." Again it happened to be a freezing day. When they got out of the jeep and started to climb under the bridge, he said, "You remain here, I want to go there alone." As he stood there viewing the scene he suddenly began stripping off his clothes. The missionary said, "Oh, son, don't do that, you'll freeze to death."

But he pushed her back, and as he stood there the cold was so violent that his body began to shake and she heard him say, "Mother, were you this cold for me . . . Mother, were you this cold for me?"

Now I want to tell you that they stripped our Savior Jesus

Christ of His dignity and honor. They hanged Him on a cross.

As I think about that scene I feel like saying, "Jesus, when You were there on the cross, were You as terror-stricken as we are about death? Were You as afraid for Your spirit to leave Your body as we are when we think about it happening to us? What did the mystery of death mean to You? How did it strike You? Why did You cry out, 'My God, My God, why hast thou forsaken Me?' Jesus, what did it really mean?"

In my heart I can hear Him saying, "My death means LIFE. It means the death of death." It means . . .

DEATH DIED THAT DAY

There on the cross something remarkable happened when Jesus said to the Father, "It is finished" (John 19:30). That is to say, "Death has Me, death has defeated Me, but I finished the work that You called Me to do." Then Jesus said, "Into thy hands I commend my spirit" (Luke 23:46).

Jesus' death and resurrection means that each of us can finish our work. At death we have only a temporary cessation of our physical existence. We can have our career. We can do it to the fullness of God's power, to the height of our ability. We can do it in the fullness of our potentiality and we can be in command of our spirit. We can commit it to God.

The resurrection of Jesus means that death is a eulogy of life. When we come to the death of one of our loved ones or the death of ourselves it is not a eulogy of death, but it's a eulogy of life. For God's eulogy is always the eulogy of life. We live in the NOW in the full meaning of life and we will take the fullness of LIFE into eternity. We will live on. So Jesus means life. His death on the cross and His resurrection means the death of death and the eulogy of life forever. It means that when you are wrestling with your problems, your weaknesses, your frustrations, your loneliness, your fears and torments, He is here this moment, in the now, saying, "Because I live, ye shall live also" (John 14:19). This is the miracle of the resurrection!

Now I want Evelyn, my wife, to share with you about a woman who attended one of our lay seminars at Oral Roberts University. She had lost her husband, hadn't she, Evelyn?

"Yes. She had lost her husband and she said, 'Mrs. Roberts, I'd like to see you for a few minutes.'

"I said, 'Fine,' and we sat down to the table to talk. She said, 'I have never felt the presence of God in my life . . . never. Since I've lost my husband, everything inside of me has dried up. I have no emotional feelings. I cannot feel sorrow. I cannot feel joy. I can't feel anything. I can't even cry.'

"So I said, 'Do you believe God loves you?'

" 'Yes,' she replied.

"I said, 'Well, let's pray about it.' I took her hands and began praying. I prayed the best I could but I couldn't feel a thing. I felt no response from her at all. Then I said, 'Let's bow our heads again for a moment. I want to ask the Lord to show us what to do. I know He loves you. I know He is concerned about you. He wants you to feel His presence.' So I bowed my head and I said, 'Lord, just give me the key to this woman.' I know in everybody there is a key, if you know how to turn it, that opens up the inner man . . . that opens up that person to God. Suddenly, I felt the woman needed love and concern so I just reached out and put my arms around her. And I said, 'Look, God loves you and I love you. I believe if we ask the Lord to do something for you He will do it, because the Lord said *seek and you shall find.*'

"We prayed again and when I looked up tears were streaming down her face. She said, 'Wow, I felt something that time!' She came to me at the end of the seminar and she said, 'Mrs.

Roberts, that prayer changed my life.' Well, it wasn't the prayer, it was God who changed her life. We found the key that opened her up, you see, because she felt somebody was concerned about her and loved her."

What God did for the woman Evelyn was talking about, He will do for you. I want you to know I believe it and I expect a miracle to happen in your life as we pray together:

Father, we come with the life message of Christ that is in the now and ask You for many miracles through Christ our Redeemer.

And now, dear friend, through our Lord Jesus Christ who is closer to you than your breath . . . who loves you more than anyone else loves you, I pray that He will heal you. I pray that He will meet the need that you're facing right now. That He will heal your broken heart . . . I pray that He will take away your deep sorrow and give you His joy. I pray that you will feel and know in your heart that God's going to work everything out. Through Jesus Christ I pray, I believe, and I expect many miracles in your life. Amen and amen.

9

How To Deal With Loneliness

I HAVE A FRIEND in Tulsa, Oklahoma, where I live, who is a federal judge. One day Allen and I were talking and he said, "Oral, do you remember the publicity we received about a certain case that I had in court recently? I sentenced that boy to six months in the penitentiary. A lot of people didn't understand that and some of them said, 'Judge, you should have sent him up for ten . . . maybe twenty years.' You know, Oral, they just don't understand. Six months in prison *is* like ten or twenty years. The funny thing is if it were their son most of those people wouldn't want me to send him up at all."

Then he said, "If this boy is put in solitary confinement, that six months will be more like sixty years."

"Why is that, Allen?"

"Well, do you know what doctors say about the person who is put in solitary confinement?"

"I'm not sure."

"Well, after the fifth day he feels completely cut off from life, from people, from everything. Then after a while, in that total isolation, his body rejects food and he begins to deteriorate. His nervous system begins to collapse and many men break down completely . . . Oral, it kills them."

You don't have to be in a prison or in solitary confinement in a prison to have this same feeling of isolation, of being lonely. We all experience it from time to time. I know I do . . . and I'm sure you do.

Psychiatrists say if a baby is not fondled, caressed and stroked, if it's not loved, it's subject to mental and physical breakdown. I am told that there's a special part of the brain that's stimulated by physical or human contact and that a human being has to have this stimulation in order to develop normally and have good health. Not only babies, but there's something in every human being that cries out for that human contact.

The other day we were with a couple and the man who was away a good deal was telling me of something that had happened between him and his wife. A few days before this he had said, "Honey, I've been wanting to hold you in my arms the last few days."

She said, "Oh, I'm so glad! Because I miss your voice and the touch of your hand when you are away."

WE NEED EACH OTHER

Sometime long ago I was with my friend, John Williams, out in western North Carolina. They built a new golf course there and they chopped it right out of the forest. All the fairways were completely surrounded by trees. We came to one green where there were four trees left around the green. These trees were isolated from the rest of the forest and they were dead. I looked at the trees on either side of the fairway and they were glorious in color, beautiful to see. At the next green I saw the same thing. I said, "John, why are these trees dead?"

He said, "Oral, we made a mistake. When we cut fairways out of the forest and left these trees alone they got lonely and died." Then he smiled and said, "You remember that Scripture which says, 'It is not good that the man should be alone' (Genesis 2:18)? Well, it applies to trees too. When trees are isolated they get lonely and die."

I CAN TAKE CARE OF MYSELF

Recently I read of a 17-year-old star athlete who took an overdose of drugs. His parents pleaded with him to go to their pastor or to their doctor but he said, "Now, look, I can handle drugs. I can take care of myself." But as the weeks and months went on, the drugs affected his play, his studies; in fact, his whole body. He couldn't eat. He began to lose weight. He didn't sleep at night. He was irritable.

One day while his mother was trying to help him he said, "Mom, I wish I were a little boy again. I wish I could go back." What he meant was that he wished he could feel her arms about him, that he could feel protected.

You know what he had done? He had reached a place where he had rejected people and God. In this rejection he took drugs but found out too late that drugs were not the answer. There in the newspaper was a picture of his tombstone, "Born 1952, Died 1970." And there's a picture of him with his words, "I can handle drugs."

Everybody says something like this one time or another. We say, "I can take care of myself . . . I can handle it." But we can't.

Not long ago my wife Evelyn and I were at a social gathering and a woman whom we had known perhaps five years came up and said, "Oh, Evelyn, Oral, I'm so glad to see you. Would you come over here just a moment?" (Now she had had a drinking problem for a long time and she had gotten to the place where she drank alone. All her friends were concerned about her. She was a member of the church.

She believed in God but somehow she had come to a point in her life where she had put alcohol in the place of people. The only way she could go to a social gathering was to drink. She felt this "turned her on" for without it she was lonely even in a crowd.) She whispered, "Oral, Evelyn, could I have an appointment with you tomorrow?"

"What is your need?" we asked.

"You know I have a drinking problem . . . and I feel so lonely—so isolated—I want you to really pray for my deliverance . . ."

"Fine, what time?" She set the time. But I had an urgency to pray immediately and I said, "Why don't we just slip over here in the corner and have that prayer now?"

"In the midst of all this? Not now—tomorrow."

Evelyn and I said, "We'll see you tomorrow," and we walked away.

Next morning at the breakfast table Evelyn said, "Oh no, oh no!" She handed me the newspaper she had been reading. I read that this woman had committed suicide during the night. I don't know when I've ever been so crushed. I knew God could have saved this woman—God could have come into her life and taken this loneliness, this isolation away . . . but she waited until it was too late.

Friend, we can take our loneliness . . . our inner alienation to the Lord. For Jesus *knows* how we feel. He *knows* what loneliness is. *It's astonishing to understand that Jesus is man.* I mean, HUMAN.

> *Himself took our infirmities, and bare our sicknesses* (Matthew 8:17).

Think of any pain that you've ever suffered, any disease that has ever fastened itself upon your body, and try to comprehend that God laid that upon Jesus and vicariously

He experienced it. Think of any human feeling that you've ever had—loneliness, despair, anger, frustration—try to understand that Jesus experienced that.

JESUS SITS WHERE WE SIT

A woman heard me say words like this on TV and she wrote back and said, "Mr. Roberts, I believed in you up until your sermon last week. Now I just can't accept you anymore because you said Jesus sits where I sit and He's gone through what I've been through. You said that He has experienced what I've experienced. I'm a divorced woman. Well, Jesus was never divorced. Now how can you say that Jesus sat where I've sat . . . that He's felt what I feel? He doesn't feel the alienation and loneliness that I feel. I no longer have a husband or a home. I don't know where I'm going to turn. How can you say that?"

I wrote back and said, "You are correct in one way. Jesus was not a divorced man. But Jesus felt alienation and loneliness. He FELT it. He walked through it and He's come to walk you through it. If you've ever had the feeling that nobody cares, He's had it. He once said:

> *The foxes have holes, and the birds of the air have nests; but the Son of man hath not where to lay his head* (Matthew 8:20).

He was born a member of a minority race. He was declared to be an illegitimate child. Some of the people in Nazareth counted the months after Mary was married and before Jesus was born, and they decided He was a bastard child. This Man has been down the road. He knows what it is to be shunned, looked down upon, talked about, and wrongly accused. He's the Son of God but He was also man."

Recently I was speaking in a chapel service at ORU. When

I finished, one young woman rushed up and said, "Oh, President Roberts, something happened to me while you spoke."

And I said, "What happened?"

She said, "Today, for the first time, I found out that God loves *me*."

I said, "Is it the first time you ever knew that?"

She said, "Yes, and it makes everything look different."

Now think about it for a moment and even say it out loud with me:

GOD LOVES ME

For the first time in her life this girl actually felt our Lord sat where she sits. She could feel Him where she was in the midst of her everyday problems.

There's a saying among the old Indians here in Oklahoma that you can never really know how the other fellow feels unless you first get into his skin and walk around in it. Listen, that's what our Savior did. He came down and got into the same skin that you walk around in, and must live out your life in. The Bible says that He suffered for us in His FLESH (1 Peter 4:1). It also says that we are actually members of His flesh (Ephesians 5:30). God says to you:

> MY CHILD, JESUS CHRIST IS SENT TO YOU IN YOUR OWN FORM AND NOW THERE IS NO DISTANCE BETWEEN YOU AND HIM, OR BETWEEN YOUR NEEDS AND HIS HEALING POWER. MY SON SAT WHERE YOU SIT AT THIS MOMENT. HE BECAME A HUMAN BEING AND ENTERED YOUR NEEDS.

The Bible says:

> *For we have not an high priest which cannot be touched with the feeling of our infirmities . . .* (Hebrews 4:15).

In all points and in every way He is touched in His heart for your temptation, trials, tribulations, pain, losses, separations, fears, sicknesses, bereavements, and sorrows. The Bible makes it very clear that the divine nature of our Lord is the Christ, but that there is another part and that is His humanness. He became a human being for man and He feels everything you feel!

I am so glad the Bible tells us about Him. Oh, how you need to pick up your Bible every day and read some of it. David said, "Thy word is a lamp unto my feet, and a light unto my path" (Psalm 119:105). Paul said, "Study to shew thyself approved unto God, a workman that needeth not to be ashamed, rightly dividing the word of truth" (2 Timothy 2:15). Don't ever get too busy to study God's Holy Word daily.

I remember as a small boy the first time I heard Will Rogers speak. We lived in Ada, Oklahoma. That year a drought came, the crops failed and farmers were being wiped out. We lived in town at the time and food was scarce. I sold newspapers on the street. One day I ran down the street shouting this headline: WILL ROGERS IS COMING! I sold lots of papers that day!

Will Rogers was able to cheer this nation up from time to time. He was well read but his humor was direct and simple. The Convention Hall in Ada was filled with people from our county; they were from all walks of life—in Sunday clothes and work clothes, blue collars and white collars. They all sat together. As a little boy, I sat there too. Will told a few funny stories then opened his billfold and gave the first money to help those who were losing everything. Soon everyone there was giving. People left the Hall that day no longer depressed. They were saying, "Will Rogers knows what we're going through. He came down here to help us with our problems."

That's what our Lord did. He came down here to cheer us, to give himself to us, to get us to open up our hearts to others. But Jesus didn't come just for one day as that big hearted Oklahoman, Will Rogers, did.

Jesus came to be with us every day
in every need
and in every way.

JESUS SAT WHERE YOU SIT TO DELIVER YOU

One time a group of men were exploring a cave when they became lost. When they did not return at the scheduled time, people called upon a man who had been reared near this cave and who knew it from end to end and top to bottom. He had walked every foot of it. He went in and found them and said, "Men, follow me and I'll walk you through the cave, then out to safety."

JESUS OFFERS YOU A TWO-FOLD PLAN

That's so much like our Lord. He comes to you with a two-fold plan:

First, He sat where you sit. He went through it.

Second, He is now beside you to walk you through your problem, your loneliness, to deliverance.

That's the important thing, you see.

WHAT IS SO BEAUTIFUL ABOUT JESUS BEING WITH YOU IS THAT HE IS WITH YOU IN HIS

PERSON . . . HE IS COME WITH THE POWER OF MIRACLES TO MEET YOUR NEEDS AND TO SAVE YOUR LIFE.

So I ask you, "Where do you sit today?" Let me tell you that Jesus Christ, our personal Lord and Savior, knows every foot of life. He has been there. He has walked every foot of it. He's felt every pain. And He not only feels it but He is ready to walk you through it. But He expects something of you. What is it? you ask.

FIRST, He says to you, DON'T GIVE UP. He says, "Don't say, I'll never come out of this."

SECOND, say, I CAN MAKE IT THROUGH MY LORD WHO HAS BEEN IN ALL OF THESE HARD PLACES BEFORE ME.

Jesus expects you to look to Him for hope and meaning in your life. And you can. He is your SOURCE. He is your TOTAL SOURCE!

Jesus said:

> *I will never leave thee, nor forsake thee* (Hebrews 13:5).

When you say, "I'm all alone and nobody cares," you are telling yourself lies. The God I'm talking about has even numbered the hairs on your head (Matthew 10:30).

He knows your name.

He knows your address.

He knows your family.

He knows every pain, frustration—every financial, physical, or spiritual need that you have.

And HE LOVES YOU.

There is no loneliness so bleak, no storm so fierce, but that you can see Jesus there with you if you will begin to look to Him as your Source . . . if you will start planting seed of your personal concern for someone else . . . and if you will begin expecting a miracle to happen to you. I mean by this that you've got to start being positive . . . you've got to start DOING something. As you do it from your heart, God will help you.

10

How You Can Rise Above Discouragement

PEOPLE SOMETIMES SAY to me, "Oral Roberts, what do you do when you get discouraged? What do you do when it just gets to be too much for you? How do you handle it when you get depressed . . . when the bills are piling up and you can't pay them . . . when you do all that you know how to do and it still doesn't work—what do you *do*? Oral Roberts, tell us like it is!"

Now some people think I never get discouraged. But they are wrong. I know what it means to get discouraged . . . to really get low. I've been so discouraged that if I'd died they would have had to jack me up to bury me. I mean, I know what I'm talking about! As one man said, I've been so low that I'd have had to climb up on a tree limb to look a snake in the eye. That's right!!

There are usually two reasons I get discouraged. First, discouragement comes when I've done my best and still I didn't get the job done . . . no matter what I did it just didn't seem to work out. There have been things that I wanted to accomplish so much it hurt . . . but it just wouldn't go. These things are in the past so all I can do with them is to give them to God.

Second, I get discouraged when I'm preparing to do something and it won't gel. Do you know what I mean? Sometimes all the pieces just don't come together . . . and it gets discouraging!!

And to be real honest and frank with you, when I get discouraged I get scared. I get that sick feeling in the pit of my stomach. Then I get irritated and I get hard to live with. I find that my words are coming out sharp and hard. Even though I try to be kind, the discouragement in my spirit comes through. My dear wife Evelyn says, "Now, honey, re member people get more from your spirit than they get from what you say . . ." And I know what she says is the truth. So then I have to get myself by the collar and say, "Oral Roberts, what does God have to say about this?" The things that I preach to others I begin to preach to myself. You see, I know my preaching works because I have to live it many, many times . . . day after day. I remind myself that . . .

GOD IS ALWAYS IN THE NOW AND HE IS NEVER *NOT* IN THE NOW

This means that I must be in the NOW . . . I must never *not* be in the now. Think about that for a moment. If you are even remotely like me, you'll have to admit that it's not easy to try a new way of doing something. We get set in our ways and we don't like to change. But this doesn't work with God. GOD IS IN THE NOW!! When you live for God you have to *learn* all the time. You never arrive! There is always something new to learn . . . and there will be till the day you die.

Jesus said:

> *Come unto me, all ye that labour and are heavy laden . . . and learn of me; for I am meek and lowly in heart: and ye shall find rest unto your souls* (Matthew 11:28,29).

LEARN OF ME! The key word in following God is *learning,* because He is always in the NOW. If you are not in the now you are either living back there somewhere in the past, trying to undo what cannot be undone, or out there somewhere in the future where you are trying to get ahead of God. And it doesn't work.

God has put this law of the NOW in everything. For example, fruit. When fruit is not ripe you have to *pull* it from the branch. If you eat the fruit while it is green it puckers your mouth as well as having other bad effects. On the other hand, if you leave it on the tree too long it will fall off and rot. Sometimes it's partially rotten when it falls off. Fruit has to be picked in the now of its ripeness. There is no other time There's just a certain time when fruit can be picked or grain can be harvested.

When you are making up your mind to do a particular thing, usually there are a few minutes or hours that that decision can be intelligently made. If you hold back, somehow you get out of step. You get confused. I believe . . .

THERE IS A *NOW* MOMENT IN EVERYBODY'S LIFE

That has a terrific influence on me. It has to do with discouragement and learning to deal with discouragement. We need to learn the way God works . . . and work with God. We need to study the life of Jesus. There is so much to be learned by what happened to Him. Remember, He was God but He was *also* man. He came down here and lived on this earth. He struggled with the same nitty-gritty problems of everyday life that you and I have to deal with.

Do you remember when Jesus was filled with the Holy Spirit at the River Jordan after He was baptized by John? It was a glorious scene as the Holy Spirit, in the form of a dove, came on Him. But Jesus left that triumphant scene to go into the wilderness to be tempted of the devil. Mark and Luke both record this incident in our Lord's life and one says that Jesus was "driven" by the Spirit into the wilderness. The other says He was "led" (Mark 1:12; Luke 4:1). They are both correct. Jesus felt a leading to go into the wilderness but He also felt God really driving Him out there . . . pushing Him. That is to say, we sometimes feel a leading to do something but we don't always do it until we are pressured.

Now why was Jesus led and/or driven into the wilderness? To have CONFLICT! The devil was there waiting for Him. The devil was not going to let Jesus be filled with the Holy Spirit without a fight. He wasn't going to just stand by and let this Man Jesus bring the gospel to the world. The devil was going to challenge Him . . . to tempt Him . . . to do everything in his power to destroy Him if possible.

If you really want to understand Jesus you can do it best by understanding yourself. If you have ever been tempted to do anything that is not right, that is exactly what Jesus felt. In any way that you've ever been tempted . . . that is the way Jesus was tempted. Perhaps you've been tempted six ways . . . or only one . . . or maybe fifteen. Chances are you've been tempted many more times and ways than that. But all the ways that every person has been tempted, Jesus was tempted. He was tempted exactly like we are.

> (He) *was in all points tempted like as we are, yet without sin* (Hebrews 4:15).

Jesus was led and/or driven into conflict . . . and that conflict continued for the rest of His life. We read where the Bible says that after this major confrontation the devil left Jesus "for a season" (Luke 4:13). This indicates that HE CAME RIGHT BACK. And he was right at Jesus' heels every step of His earthly ministry.

Let me tell you something, there is no such thing as winning a one-time total victory over the devil in this mortal life. There is no such thing. He is going to hit you until the last breath leaves your body. He is going to tempt you as long as you have any feeling in your human existence. He is going to be after you.

The only good thing about this is that if the devil is after you . . . he hasn't got you!! That's a real good thought. Whenever you say, "The devil is really after me today," you are saying a very positive thing. You are saying something very important because this means the devil doesn't own you. He doesn't possess you. But he is after you . . . he is striking out at you. You've got to understand one thing about the devil—he doesn't like you. And he isn't ever going to like you. He is going to dislike you as long as you live. He is after your eternal soul to destroy you forever.

Now that is important to realize. But it is more important to know . . . in your heart—deep in your inner man . . . that GOD LIKES YOU. GOD LOVES YOU. AND HE IS ALWAYS GOING TO LOVE YOU.

Even when you don't like yourself, God loves you.

When you are miserable and afraid, God loves you.

When you fail, God loves you.

When you are discouraged . . . when you've hit the bottom and there is no place else to go . . . GOD LOVES YOU.

Sometime ago the renowned Dr. Karl Barth visited the United States. He was lecturing at various seminaries and churches. After he had spoken at one seminary time was given for questions and answers. One of the young seminarians stood to his feet and asked, "Dr. Barth, in all of your study, what is the greatest theological truth that you have ever learned?"

Thoughtfully Dr. Barth said, *The greatest truth is this . . . and I learned it when I was a young child:*

JESUS LOVES ME THIS I KNOW
FOR THE BIBLE TELLS ME SO

Some of the most beautiful things that God has ever done for human beings have been when those individuals have been discouraged. *For example, the only time angels cooked for a person was for a discouraged man.* His name was Elijah. The interesting thing is that Elijah got in this discouraged state right after he had done one of the biggest things that God ever asked him to do (1 Kings 18). He had just confronted the prophets of Baal on Mount Carmel. He told the people of Israel to be there. He challenged the prophets of Baal: "Build an altar to your god, put a sacrifice on it and then pray and ask your god to consume it with fire. I'll do the same thing. And the god that answers by fire, the same shall be God." The prophets of Baal prayed all day and there was no answer. Elijah made it even harder for himself by having barrels of water poured on his sacrifice but it was not hard for God. Elijah prayed once and fire fell from heaven and consumed the sacrifice and also the water around it. A great victory was wrought for God that day.

But only a few hours later we find Elijah sitting under a juniper tree completely discouraged . . . feeling as discouraged as a person can feel (1 Kings 19:4). This tells me something. Sometimes we get the most discouraged after we've had our biggest successes. This tells me: "Oral, the devil doesn't like you. There is nothing that you are going to do that's going to make you a 'good guy' with him. You may do something for God and you are very pleased with it. You think people will pat you on the back. And some will. But some of them are going to kick you harder after you've done well than if you had failed. This is the devil's strategy."

The Bible says:

> *He that shall endure unto the end, the same shall be saved* (Mark 13:13).

You can't be human and not be discouraged. Even our Lord tasted it. How do you think He was feeling on the cross when He said, "My God, my God, why hast thou forsaken me?" (Mark 15:34).

When I deal with people who are in serious trouble, do you know the first thing they say? "*Why? Why* has this happened to me? What have I done to deserve it?" And if they continue asking this kind of question, it's always the sign of a loser. The sign of a winner is, "How am I going to get out of this?" The sign of a loser is, "Why did God do me this way?"

Now God owns me and let me tell you something, that makes a lot of difference. He owns me whether I make mistakes or not. He's got me on His hands. I made up my mind I'm going to serve God whether I'm sick or well, happy or unhappy, wealthy or poor. Succeed or fail, I'm going to serve God. He's got me. He's got me when I'm discouraged. He's got me when I have victory. The Man's got me.

This Jesus can come to us right where we hurt . . when we are down. He gets right down where the need or the problem or the discouragement is. And then He is able to DO something about it.

When Jesus met a person with a problem, He said:

BE OF GOOD CHEER . . . OR CHEER UP!

Do you realize it's almost impossible not to have a bad attitude when things keep going wrong? It is nearly impossible not to have a bad attitude when things just keep pressing down on you. You can go along sweet and satisfied and love everybody and get along and feel good. But let the tables turn and you have days and days and days of bad things and bad feelings happening. And if you don't watch, you will develop a bad attitude. I know because I've done it. I'm saying that just to be honest.

The other day I received a letter from one of our students. It read:

> Dear President Roberts:
>
> I have wanted to write you for a long time, first to thank you . . . for this school and God's people here that God has used to give me the new self and the new mind which God's Word speaks about so often. When I first came to ORU I had an inferiority complex so bad I hated myself and thought God made a mistake when He created me. My world revolved around problems, inferior feelings, and a horrible negative attitude which saw no good in anything!

As I read this letter the Scripture kept coming to me, "Confess your faults one to another, and pray one for another, that ye may be healed" (James 5:16). I'm sure there's a great healing coming to this girl, if it hasn't already come, because she has confessed her need. She continued:

> Through the sharings in chapel and the Holy Spirit class and through teachers and friends here at ORU, God has begun to deal with me in a real way. Oh, how I thank Him and want Him to continue His work. I actually get amazed when I look at myself and now realize what He's done. He is able to do exceedingly abundantly above all I can ask or think.

Now she's sort of pulling out of the slump and getting up the hill. I am seeing the Scripture come alive. Then she says:

> ORU has opened up a new life and a new world for me by showing, sharing, and teaching me how the Lord is working in me. I really get excited when I think of my miracle.

I've just got to stop there. She says she gets excited when she thinks about "my" miracle. Somebody said:

A MIRACLE NEVER HAPPENS UNTIL IT HAPPENS TO YOU

You may hear about all the miracles in the Bible and in other people's lives but there's nothing to a miracle until it happens to you. It's never real until it's real to you. She went on to say:

> Now I have the desire to tell the other droopy-headed kids, with all their frustrations, of my new hope.
>
> The second thing is a burden I would like for you to pray about. My dad is awfully sick. He has a heart condition and something else with a long medical name. To put it short, the doctors say he will gradually lose the ability to walk and talk. His leg usage gets less and less, but
>
> *God is bigger than our problems.*
>
> And I have figured if God could make hearts, why couldn't He fix them and the whole human body? I realize God has a purpose, but my dad sort of lacks faith. Not my mother though. It's hard to explain, but I know you understand what I mean. My mother usually has a witness because of the strength of God in her to endure these situations.

President Roberts, will you pray for them? My mother gets your letters and every time she writes you of my daddy she thanks God I am here at ORU. Yet I feel bad because I'm not with her helping with Daddy. But I know God called me here because of what He's doing. Anyway . . .

God can do more than I can.

He can love them more and help them more and I am claiming a miracle but just needed to share it with somebody.

I thank you for taking time to listen. It makes me feel much better now that I know more prayer is going up.

—Much love and prayers always

I get a lot of letters like that. I know it's tough for you to believe but I have a feeling for my partners that I can't always put into words. However, I'm a grateful person. I'm always grateful for people who help me, especially the people who have helped me build this ministry. You know, I really get a lump in my throat when I think about it. So let me say to you—and I get the echo of it back in my own heart —"Cheer up." Now I want to tell you of a time when Jesus said this to His disciples. Here's what happened:

The disciples were rowing across the Sea of Galilee in the night. They ran into a storm. The winds were blowing, the waves were rolling high, the water was sucking at the little boat, and the timbers began to pop. The disciples were rubbing elbows with death and they screamed out with fear. Then, the Bible says, while Christ was on the mountain praying . . .

He saw them toiling in rowing; for the wind was contrary (Mark 6:48).

The mind of Jesus penetrated the blackness of the terrible storm. He saw the little boat tossed by the waves. He heard the anguished cry of the men. That's hard to believe, isn't it? Particularly when you are so hemmed in by your problems, so desperate in your need, so discouraged that you begin to wonder if God exists? If He's even within a million miles of you? Well, here in this story the storm struck suddenly and the disciples were face-to-face with death.

You know, it can happen so suddenly—the burdens, the struggles, the torments of life strike quickly—and then we wonder, WHERE IS GOD? But the Bible says:

"He saw them" . . . *them.*

Yes, sir, from the mountain where Jesus was praying He looked down on the sea where the disciples were rubbing elbows with death, crying out in fear, and He saw them. He heard them. He felt them—THEM.

This shows us that God has made provision for us.

WHY DIDN'T THE DISCIPLES RECOGNIZE JESUS?

Why didn't the disciples recognize Him? Why was He shrouded in a cloak of misunderstanding? Why did they call Him a ghost? Why did they seemingly first think of the occult? Why weren't they able to see Him in His physical form? They failed to recognize Him because they were not expecting Him to appear. This could be your trouble today. Perhaps you are not getting your miracles because your mind is still on the problem, on the fear gnawing at your insides, and you are not OPENING YOUR MIND to miracles.

> *You must put in seed faithfully . . . look to God as your only real and faithful Source . . . and expect the miracles that you need!*

God performed miracles through Jesus on the front streets and the dusty roads, in the fields and houses and vineyards and shops, and then on the waters of the Holy Land. He did it because many people finally looked beyond their sicknesses and fears, discouragement and loneliness and financial needs —because they started EXPECTING Him to meet their needs. Because they finally fixed their eyes upon the real Source for their lives. It still works like that TODAY because Jesus operates best in a feeling of expectancy you have about Him.

Now, I want to give to you the secret of how to rise above discouragement. I have discovered that as long as I follow my Lord in the 3 MIRACLE KEYS OF SEED-FAITH, I can have miracle after miracle . . . I can find the solution to my problems.

Key No. 1. A commitment to look to Him as my Savior and as MY SOURCE for my total supply . . .

Key No. 2. A commitment that I must seed for my miracles by giving first—by acts of loving service to others first—and doing it in joy . . .

Key No. 3. A commitment to EXPECT MIRACLES from the seeds of faith I put into God's great work . . . and to expect a new miracle every day!